Using Node.js for UI Testing

Learn how to easily automate testing of your web apps using Node.js, Zombie.js, and Mocha

Pedro Teixeira

PUBLISHING

BIRMINGHAM - MUMBAI

Using Node.js for UI Testing

First published: March 2013

Production Reference: 1150313

Published by Packt Publishing Ltd.
Livery Place
35 Livery Street
Birmingham B3 2PB, UK..

ISBN 978-1-78216-052-6

www.packtpub.com

Cover Image by Suresh Mogre (suresh.mogre.99@gmail.com)

Credits

Author
Pedro Teixeira

Reviewers
Ollie Bennett

David Mark Clements

Acquisition Editor
Joanne Fitzpatrick

Commissioning Editor
Priyanka Shah

Technical Editor
Chirag Jani

Copy Editors
Brandt D'Mello

Insiya Morbiwala

Alfida Paiva

Laxmi Subramanian

Ruta Waghmare

Project Coordinator
Esha Thakker

Proofreader
Dan McMahon

Indexer
Tejal R. Soni

Production Coordinator
Conidon Miranda

Cover Work
Conidon Miranda

About the Author

Pedro Teixeira is a prolific open source programmer and author of many Node.js modules. Since graduating in Software Engineering over 14 years ago, he has been a consultant, a programmer, and an active and internationally known Node.js community member.

He is a founding partner of The Node Firm and a Senior Programmer at Nodejitsu Inc., the leading Node.js platform as a service (PaaS) provider. He is also the author of the popular Node Tuts screencasts and two books about Node.js, namely, *Hands-on Node.js (self-published)* and *Professional Node.js (Wrox Publication)*.

When he was ten years old, his father taught him how to program a ZX Spectrum, and since then he has never wanted to stop. He taught himself how to program his father's Apple IIc and then entered the PC era. During college he was introduced to the world of UNIX and open source, and became seriously addicted to it. In his professional life, he has developed systems and products built with Visual Basic, C, C++, Java, PHP, Ruby, and JavaScript for big telecom companies, banks, hotel chains, and others.

He has been a Node.js enthusiast since the very beginning, having authored many applications and also many well-known modules such as Fugue, Alfred.js, Carrier, Nock, and others.

I would like to thank my amazing wife Susana for her support and resilience, you have always been a corner stone and been there for me.

I'd also like to thank the amazing JavaScript and Node.js community for being so enthusiastic and innovative, always taking everyone along on crazy rides, being at the fulcrum of expanding the reach and capabilities of programmers.

About the Reviewers

Ollie Bennett is a technical consultant based in London, with a passion for playing with the latest technologies. After completing a Master's degree in Theoretical Physics, he focused his attention on Web development, and maintains a portfolio of websites. Node.js and other recent JavaScript advancements are forming an ever increasing part of his interests.

His personal website address is `http://olliebennett.co.uk/`.

David Mark Clements is a Web entrepreneur residing in Northern Ireland. From a very early age he was fascinated with programming and computers. He first learned BASIC on one of the many Ataris he had accumulated by the age of nine. He learned JavaScript at the age of 12, moving into Linux administration and PHP as a teenager.

Now (as a twenty something), he enjoys working with CSS and HTML, but most of all he enjoys JavaScript—both in the browser and using Node. He wrote *Node Cookbook (Packt Publishing)*, a selection of recipes to help coders master the art of asynchronous server-side JavaScript using Node.

Professionally, David is a freelancer who builds responsive websites and web apps for both enterprise and non-governmental organizations, and offers JavaScript/Node training.

You can follow David on Twitter at `@davidmarkclem`.

www.PacktPub.com

Support files, eBooks, discount offers and more

You might want to visit www.PacktPub.com for support files and downloads related to your book.

Did you know that Packt offers eBook versions of every book published, with PDF and ePub files available? You can upgrade to the eBook version at www.PacktPub.com and as a print book customer, you are entitled to a discount on the eBook copy. Get in touch with us at service@packtpub.com for more details.

At www.PacktPub.com, you can also read a collection of free technical articles, sign up for a range of free newsletters and receive exclusive discounts and offers on Packt books and eBooks.

http://PacktLib.PacktPub.com

Do you need instant solutions to your IT questions? PacktLib is Packt's online digital book library. Here, you can access, read and search across Packt's entire library of books.

Why Subscribe?

- Fully searchable across every book published by Packt
- Copy and paste, print and bookmark content
- On demand and accessible via web browser

Free Access for Packt account holders

If you have an account with Packt at www.PacktPub.com, you can use this to access PacktLib today and view nine entirely free books. Simply use your login credentials for immediate access.

Table of Contents

Preface

Automating tests for user interfaces has always been the holy grail of programming. Now, using Zombie.js and Mocha you can quickly create and run your tests, making it simple to test even the smallest changes. Increase your confidence in the code and minimize the number of times you have to use a real browser while you develop.

Using Node.js for UI Testing is a quick yet thorough guide on how to automatically test your web app, keeping it rock-solid and bug-free. You will learn how to simulate complex user behavior and verify that your application behaves correctly.

You will create a web app in Node.js that uses complex user interactions and AJAX; by the end of this book you will be able to fully test it from the command line. Then you will start creating the user interface tests for this application using Mocha as a framework and Zombie.js as a headless browser.

You will also create a complete test suite, module by module, testing simple and complex user interactions.

What this book covers

Chapter 1, Getting started with Zombie.js, helps you to understand how Zombie.js works and what types of applications can be tested with it.

Chapter 2, Creating a Simple Web App, explains how to create a simple web app using Node.js, CouchDB, and Flatiron.js.

Chapter 3, Installing Zombie.js and Mocha, teaches you about creating the base structure of a test environment for a web application using Zombie.js and Mocha.

Chapter 4, Understanding Mocha, helps you to understand how you can use Mocha to create and run asynchronous tests.

Chapter 5, Manipulating the Zombie Browser, explains how Zombie.js is used to create a simulated browser that can load an HTML document and perform actions on it.

Chapter 6, Testing Interactions, explains how to trigger events in a document and how to test the results of document manipulations.

Chapter 7, Debugging, teaches you how to inspect the internal state of your application by using the Zombie browser object and some other techniques.

Chapter 8, Testing AJAX, is not present in the book but is available as a free download at the following link:

```
http://www.packtpub.com/sites/default/files/downloads/0526_8_
testingajax.pdf
```

What you need for this book

To use this book you will need a PC running a modern mainstream operating system such as Windows, Mac, or Linux.

Who this book is for

This book is for programmers who use and somewhat understand JavaScript, especially having some experience with event-driven programming. For instance, if you have used JavaScript in the context of a web page for setting up event callbacks and making AJAX calls, you will experience a smoother learning curve. Alternatively, some experience in using Node.js will also ease the learning curve, but is not an absolute requirement.

Conventions

In this book, you will find a number of styles of text that distinguish between different kinds of information. Here are some examples of these styles, and an explanation of their meaning.

Code words in text, database table names, folder names, filenames, file extensions, pathnames, dummy URLs, user input, and Twitter handles are shown as follows: " To access a CouchDB database from Node you will use a library called nano."

A block of code is set as follows:

```
browser.visit('http://localhost:8080/form', function() {
  browser
    .fill('Name', 'Pedro Teixeira')
    .select('Born', '1975')
    .check('Agree with terms and conditions')
    .pressButton('Submit', function() {
      assert.equal(browser.location.pathname, '/success');
      assert.equal(browser.text('#message'),
        'Thank you for submitting this form!');
    });
});
```

When we wish to draw your attention to a particular part of a code block, the relevant lines or items are set in bold:

```
"scripts": {
  "test": "mocha test/users.js",
  "start": "node app.js"
},...
```

Any command-line input or output is written as follows:

```
$ npm install
...
mocha@1.4.2 node_modules/mocha
...


zombie@1.4.1 node_modules/zombie
...
```

New terms and **important words** are shown in bold. Words that you see on the screen, in menus or dialog boxes for example, appear in the text like this: "clicking the **Next** button moves you to the next screen".

 Warnings or important notes appear in a box like this.

 Tips and tricks appear like this.

Reader feedback

Feedback from our readers is always welcome. Let us know what you think about this book—what you liked or may have disliked. Reader feedback is important for us to develop titles that you really get the most out of.

To send us general feedback, simply send an e-mail to feedback@packtpub.com, and mention the book title via the subject of your message.

If there is a topic that you have expertise in and you are interested in either writing or contributing to a book, see our author guide on www.packtpub.com/authors.

Customer support

Now that you are the proud owner of a Packt book, we have a number of things to help you to get the most from your purchase.

Downloading the example code

You can download the example code files for all Packt books you have purchased from your account at http://www.packtpub.com. If you purchased this book elsewhere, you can visit http://www.packtpub.com/support and register to have the files e-mailed directly to you.

Errata

Although we have taken every care to ensure the accuracy of our content, mistakes do happen. If you find a mistake in one of our books—maybe a mistake in the text or the code—we would be grateful if you would report this to us. By doing so, you can save other readers from frustration and help us improve subsequent versions of this book. If you find any errata, please report them by visiting http://www.packtpub.com/submit-errata, selecting your book, clicking on the **errata submission form** link, and entering the details of your errata. Once your errata are verified, your submission will be accepted and the errata will be uploaded on our website, or added to any list of existing errata, under the Errata section of that title. Any existing errata can be viewed by selecting your title from http://www.packtpub.com/support.

Piracy

Piracy of copyright material on the Internet is an ongoing problem across all media. At Packt, we take the protection of our copyright and licenses very seriously. If you come across any illegal copies of our works, in any form, on the Internet, please provide us with the location address or website name immediately so that we can pursue a remedy.

Please contact us at copyright@packtpub.com with a link to the suspected pirated material.

We appreciate your help in protecting our authors, and our ability to bring you valuable content.

Questions

You can contact us at questions@packtpub.com if you are having a problem with any aspect of the book, and we will do our best to address it.

1
Getting Started with Zombie.js

"Zombie.js is a lightweight framework for testing client-side JavaScript code in a simulated environment. No browser required."

This definition is from the *Zombie.js* documentation at `http://zombie.labnotes.org`

Automating tests for your web application is crucial to having a quality product, but doing it properly can be a painful experience. That is why most of the time this part of the project never gets implemented. Developers either limit themselves to testing the underlying business logic and control flow in isolation, or, if they really want to test the user interface, must resort to complicated setups where you somehow connect to real browsers and command them using remote scripts.

Zombie.js provides a fast and easy alternative to this scenario, enabling you to easily and quickly create automated tests for your web application just by using JavaScript.

The topics covered in this chapter are:

- A brief history of software testing
- Understanding the server-side DOM
- How Zombie.js works internally

By the end of this chapter, you should understand how Zombie.js works and what types of applications can be tested using it.

A brief history of software and user interface testing

Software testing is a necessary activity for gathering information about the quality of a certain product or a service. In the traditional software development cycle, this activity had been delegated to a team whose sole job was to find problems in the software. This type of testing would be required if a generic product was being sold to a domestic end user or if a company was buying a licensed operating system.

In most custom-built pieces of software, the testing team has the responsibility of manually testing the software, but often the client has to do the acceptance testing in which he or she has to make sure that the software behaves as expected.

Every time someone in these teams finds a new problem in the software, the development team has to fix the software and put it back in the testing loop one more time. This implies that the cost and time required to deliver a final version of the software increases every time a bug is found. Furthermore, the later in the development process the problem is found, the more it will impact the final cost of the product.

Also, the way software is delivered has changed in the last few years; the Web has enabled us to make the delivery of software and its upgrade easy, shortening the time between when new functionality is developed and when it is put in use. But once you have delivered the first version of a product and have a few customers using it, you can face a dilemma; fewer updates can mean the product quickly becomes obsolete. On the other hand, introducing many changes in the software increases the chance of something going wrong and your software becoming faulty, which may drive customers away.

There are many versions and iterations over how a development process can mitigate the risk of shipping a faulty product and increase the chances of new functionalities to be delivered on time, and for the overall product to meet a certain quality standard, but all people involved in building software must agree that the sooner you catch a bug, the better.

This means that you should catch the problems early on, preferably in the development cycle. Unfortunately, completely testing the software by hand every time the software changes, would be costly. The solution here is to automate the tests in order to maximize the test coverage (the percentage of the application code that is tested and the possible input variations) and minimize the time it takes to run each test. If your tests take just a few seconds to run, you can afford to run them every time you make a single change in the code base.

Enter the automation era

Test automation has been around for some years, even before the Web was around. As soon as **graphical user interfaces (GUIs)** started to become mainstream, the tools that allowed you to record, build, and run automated tests against a GUI started appearing. Since there were many languages and GUI libraries for building applications, many tools that covered some of these started showing up. Generally they allowed you to record a testing session that you could later recreate automatically. In this session, you could automate the pointer to click on things (buttons, checkboxes, places on a window, and so on), select values (from a select box, for instance), and input keyboard actions and test the results.

All of these tools were fairly complex to operate and, worst of all, most of them were technology-specific.

But, if you're building a web-based application that uses HTML and JavaScript, you have better alternatives. The most well known of these is likely to be Selenium, which allows you to record, change, and run testing scripts against all the major browsers.

You can run tests using Selenium, but you need at least one browser for Selenium to attach itself to, in order to load and run the tests. If you run the tests with as many browsers as you possibly can, you will be able to guarantee that your application behaves correctly across all of them. But since Selenium plugs into a browser and commands it, running all the tests for a considerably complex application in as many browsers as possible can take some time, and the last thing you want is to not run the tests as often as possible.

Unit tests versus integration tests

Generally you can divide automated tests into two categories, namely unit tests and integration tests.

- **Unit tests**: These tests are where you select a small subset of your application—such as a class or a specific object—and test the interface the class or object provides to the rest of the application. In this way, you can isolate a specific component and make sure it behaves as expected so that other components in the application can use it safely.

- **Integration tests**: These tests are where individual components are combined together and tested as a working group. During these tests, you interact and manipulate the user interface that in turn interacts with the underlying blocks of your application. The kind of testing you do with Zombie.js falls in this category.

What Zombie.js is

Zombie.js allows you to run these tests without a real web browser. Instead, it uses a simulated browser where it stores the HTML code and runs the JavaScript you may have in your HTML page. This means that an HTML page doesn't need to be displayed, saving precious time that would otherwise be occupied rendering it.

You can then use Zombie.js to conduct this simulated browser into loading pages and, once a page is loaded, doing certain actions and observing the results. And you can do all this using JavaScript, never having to switch languages between your client code and your test scripts.

Understanding the server-side DOM

Zombie.js runs on top of Node.js (`http://nodejs.org`), a platform where you can easily build networking servers using JavaScript. It runs on top of Google's fast V8 JavaScript engine that also powers their Chrome browsers.

> At the time of writing, V8 implements the JavaScript ECMA 3 standard and part of the ECMA 5 standard. Not all browsers implement all the features of all the versions of the JavaScript standards equally. This means that even if your tests pass in Zombie.js, it doesn't mean they will pass for all the target browsers.

On top of Node.js, there is a third-party module named JSDOM (`https://npmjs.org/package/jsdom`) that allows you to parse an HTML document and use an API on top of a representation of that document; this allows you to query and manipulate it. The API provided is the standard **Document Object Model** (**DOM**).

All browsers implement a subset of the DOM standard, which has been dictated as a set of recommendations by a working group inside the **World Wide Web Consortium** (**W3C**). They have three levels of recommendations. JSDOM implements all three.

Web applications, directly or indirectly (by using tools such as jQuery), use this browser-provided DOM API to query and manipulate the document, enabling you to create browser applications that have complex behavior. This means that by using JSDOM you automatically support any JavaScript libraries that most modern browsers support.

Downloading the example code

You can download the example code files for all Packt books you have purchased from your account at http://www.packtpub.com. If you purchased this book elsewhere, you can visit http://www.packtpub.com/support and register to have the files e-mailed directly to you.

Zombie.js is your headless browser

On top of Node.js and JSDOM lies Zombie.js. Zombie.js provides browser-like functionality and an API you can use for testing. For instance, a typical use of Zombie.js would be to open a browser, ask for a certain URL to be loaded, fill some values on a form, and submit it, and then query the resulting document to see if a success message is present.

To make it more concrete, here is a simple example of what the code for a simple Zombie.js test may look like:

```
browser.visit('http://localhost:8080/form', function() {
  browser
    .fill('Name', 'Pedro Teixeira')
    .select('Born', '1975')
    .check('Agree with terms and conditions')
    .pressButton('Submit', function() {
      assert.equal(browser.location.pathname, '/success');
      assert.equal(browser.text('#message'),
        'Thank you for submitting this form!');
    });
});
```

Here you are making typical use of Zombie.js: to load an HTML page containing a form; filling that form and submitting it; and then verifying that the result is successful.

Zombie.js may not only be used for testing your web app but also by applications that need to behave like browsers, such as HTML scrapers, crawlers, and all sorts of HTML bots.

If you are going to use Zombie.js to do any of these activities, please be a good Web citizen and use it ethically.

Summary

Creating automated tests is a vital part of the development process of any software application. When creating web applications using HTML, JavaScript, and CSS, you can use Zombie.js to create a set of tests; these tests load, query, manipulate, and provide inputs to any given web page.

Given that Zombie.js simulates a browser and does not depend on the actual rendering of the HTML page, the tests run much faster than they would if you instrumented a real browser. Thus it is possible for you to run these tests whenever you make any small changes to your application.

Zombie.js runs on top of Node.js, uses JSDOM to provide a DOM API on top of any HTML document, and simulates browser-like functionalities with a simple API that you can use to create your tests using JavaScript.

2

Creating a Simple Web App

By the time you reach the end of this chapter, you should be able to create a simple web application using Node.js, CouchDB, and Flatiron.

The topics covered in this chapter are:

- Setting up Node and Flatiron
- Creating and processing a user form

Defining the requirements of our web app

Before we dive too much into the Zombie.js world, we need to create a target for our tests, that is, a web application that provides a to-do list. This is the set of top-level requirements for such an application:

- A user can sign up for the service for which he should provide an e-mail address as username and a password. By providing the username and the password, the user can create an authenticated session that will identify him throughout further interactions.
- The user can create a to-do item.
- The user can view a list of to-dos.
- The user can remove a to-do item.

To implement this application we will use Node.js, a platform for building networking applications in JavaScript that Zombie.js also uses. We'll also use Flatiron, a set of components that will help you in building a web application on top of Node.js.

In the interest of keeping things simple, we're building our application in Node.js. However, Zombie.js is suitable for testing applications built with any framework utilizing a dynamic HTTP server.

Also, bear in mind that the goal of building this web application is not to show you how to build a web app, but to provide a working application on a known and simple domain that we can use as the subject of our tests.

In the next sections you'll learn how to install Node.js and Flatiron and how to create your to-do application server.

Setting up Node.js and Flatiron

If you don't have the latest version of Node.js installed, you will need to install it. You will need Node.js for several reasons. Our web application will use Flatiron, which runs on top of Node.js. You will also need to use the **Node Package Manager** (**NPM**), which comes bundled with Node. Finally, you will need Node.js to install and run your Zombie.js tests.

Installing Node.js

1. To install Node.js head out to the nodejs.org website.

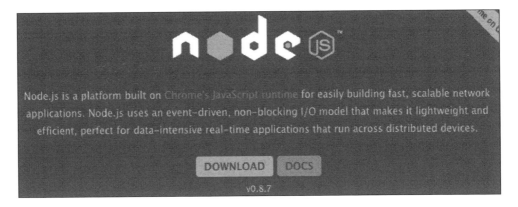

2. Then click on the **Download** button, which should open the following page:

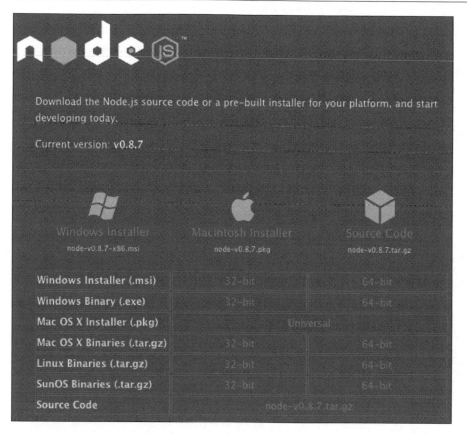

3. If you're running a Windows or a Macintosh system, click on the respective installer icon. That should download and start up the graphical installer.

Installing Node from the source code

If you're not running one of these systems and you are on a Unix-like system, you can install Node.js from the source code by following these steps:

1. Click on the source code icon, which will start downloading the source code tarball. Once downloaded, expand it using the terminal:

```
$ tar xvfz node-v0.8.7.tar.gz
```

Navigate to the created dir:

```
$ cd node-v0.8.7
```

2. Configure it:

```
$ ./configure
```

3. Build it:

```
$ make
```

4. And finally install it:

```
$ make install
```

If you don't have sufficient permissions to copy the node binaries to the final destination, you will need to prefix your command with `sudo`:

```
$ sudo make install
```

5. Now you should have Node.js installed on your system. Try running it:

```
$ node -v
v0.8.7
```

6. Now let's try to open the Node command line and type something:

```
$ node
> console.log('Hello World!');
```

7. If you press *Enter* now, you should get the following output:

```
...
> Hello World!
```

8. By installing Node.js, you also installed its faithful companion NPM, the Node Package Manager. You can try invoking it from the terminal:

```
$ npm -v
1.1.48
```

Installing Flatiron and starting your application

Now you need to install the Flatiron framework so you can start building your application.

1. Use NPM to download and install Flatiron as follows:

```
$ npm install -g flatiron
```

 Again, if you don't have enough permissions to install Flatiron, run the last command prefixed by `sudo`.

This installs Flatiron globally, making the `flatiron` command-line utility available.

2. Now you should step in a directory that will have the application code. You can then create the basic scaffolding for your web app by executing the following command:

```
$ flatiron create todo
```

3. After prompting you for the name of the author, the app description, and the homepage (which is optional), it will create a directory named `todo` containing the base for your application code. Step into that directory using the following command:

```
$ cd todo
```

There you will find two files and three folders:

```
$ tree
.
├── app.js
├── config
│   └── config.json
├── lib
├── package.json
└── test
```

One of these files, `package.json` contains the application manifest, which, among other fields, contains the packages that your application depends on. For now you're going to remove the `devDependencies` field from that file.

You'll also need to add a dependency for the package named `plates`, which will be used for changing HTML templates on the fly.

Also, you will be serving some static files that won't need any modification. For that you will use a package named `node-static`, which you also need to add to the dependencies list of your application manifest.

By now your `package.json` should look something like this:

```
{
  "description": "To-do App",
  "version": "0.0.0",
  "private": true,
  "dependencies": {
    "union": "0.3.0",
    "flatiron": "0.2.8",
    "plates": "0.4.x",
```

```
      "node-static": "0.6.0"
  },
  "scripts": {
    "test": "vows --spec",
    "start": "node app.js"
  },
  "name": "todo",
  "author": "Pedro",
  "homepage": ""
}
```

4. Next, install those dependencies by using the following:

```
$ npm install
```

This will install all the dependencies in a local `node_modules` directory and should output something like the following:

```
union@0.3.0 node_modules/union
├── qs@0.4.2
└── pkginfo@0.2.3

flatiron@0.2.8 node_modules/flatiron
├── pkginfo@0.2.3
├── director@1.1.0
├── optimist@0.3.4 (wordwrap@0.0.2)
├── broadway@0.2.5 (eventemitter2@0.4.9, cliff@0.1.8, utile@0.1.2,
nconf@0.6.4, winston@0.6.2)
└── prompt@0.2.6 (revalidator@0.1.2, read@1.0.4, utile@0.1.3,
winston@0.6.2)

plates@0.4.6 node_modules/plates

node-static@0.6.0 node_modules/node-static
```

 You don't have to worry about this, since Node will be able to pick up these dependencies automatically.

5. Now you can try to start up your app:

```
$ node app.js
```

If you open a browser and point it to `http://localhost:3000`, you will get the following response:

```
{"hello":"world"}
```

Creating your to-do app

Now that you have a Flatiron "hello world" example running, you need to extend it so that our to-do application takes shape. For this you will need to create and change some files. If you ever get lost, you can always refer to the chapter's source code. Also, for your reference, there is a complete list of the project files included at the end of this chapter.

Setting up the database

As in any real application, you will need a reliable way to persist data. Here we will use CouchDB, the open-source and document-oriented database. You can either choose to install CouchDB locally or use a service over the Internet, such as Iris Couch.

If you choose to install CouchDB on your local development machine, you can head out and visit `http://couchdb.apache.org/`, click on **Download** and follow the instructions.

If you prefer to simply use CouchDB over the Internet, you can head out to `http://www.iriscouch.com/`, click on the **Sign Up Now** button and fill the registration form. You should have a running CouchDB instance in a matter of seconds.

As of this writing, Iris Couch is a service that is free for small databases with low traffic, which makes it ideal for prototyping an application such as this one.

Accessing CouchDB from Node

To access a CouchDB database from Node we will use a library called `nano`, which you will add to the dependencies section of your `package.json` file:

```json
{
  "description": "To-do App",
  "version": "0.0.0",
  "private": true,
  "dependencies": {
    "union": "0.3.0",
    "flatiron": "0.2.8",
    "plates": "0.4.6",
    "node-static": "0.6.0",
    "nano": "3.3.0"
  },
  "scripts": {
    "test": "vows --spec",
    "start": "node app.js"
  },
  "name": "todo",
  "author": "Pedro",
  "homepage": ""
}
```

Now you can install this missing dependency by running the following command at the root of your application:

```
$ npm install
nano@3.3.0 node_modules/nano
├── errs@0.2.3
├── request@2.9.203
└── follow@0.8.0 (request@2.2.9request@2.2.9)
```

This installs `nano` inside the `node_modules` folder, making it available for help while building this app.

To actually connect to the database, you need to define the CouchDB server URL. If you're running CouchDB locally, the URL should be similar to `http://127.0.0.1:5984`. If you are running CouchDB in Iris Couch or a similar service, your URL will be similar to `https://mytodoappcouchdb.iriscouch.com`.

In any of these cases, if you need to access using a username and a password, you should encode these in the URL, `http://username:password@mytodoappcouchdb.iriscouch.com`

This URL should now be entered into a configuration file under `config/config.json`, under the `couchdb` key:

```
{
   "couchdb": "http://localhost:5984"
}
```

Next, encapsulate the access to the database by providing a simple module under `lib/couchdb.js`:

```
var nano = require('nano'),
    config = require('../config/config.json');

module.exports = nano(config.couchdb);
```

This module will be used to get a CouchDB server object instead of repeating the `config` and `nano` dance several times throughout the code.

Application layout

As many websites do nowadays, we will be using the Twitter Bootstrap framework to help us in getting the website look and feel minimal yet presentable. For that you will head out to the Bootstrap website `http://twitter.github.com/bootstrap/` and click on the **Download Bootstrap** button:

You will get a zip file, which you should expand into the local `public` folder, ending up with these files:

```
$ tree public/
public/
├── css
│   ├── bootstrap-responsive.css
│   ├── bootstrap-responsive.min.css
│   ├── bootstrap.css
│   └── bootstrap.min.css
├── img
```

```
|   ├── glyphicons-halflings-white.png
|   └── glyphicons-halflings.png
└── js
    ├── bootstrap.js
    └── bootstrap.min.js
```

You will also need to add jQuery into the mix since Bootstrap depends on it. Download jQuery from `http://jquery.com` and name it `public/js/jquery.min.js`.

Developing the frontend

Now that we have Bootstrap and jQuery installed, it's time to create the frontend of our application.

First we will set up the layout HTML template, which defines the outer structure for all the pages. For hosting all the templates, we will have a directory named `templates`, containing the following under `templates/layout.html`:

```html
<html>
  <head>
    <meta http-equiv="Content-Type" content="text/html; charset=utf-8" />
    <title id="title"></title>
    <link href="/css/bootstrap.min.css" rel="stylesheet" />
  </head>
  <body>

    <section role="main" class="container">

      <div id="messages"></div>

      <div id="main-body"></div>

    </section>

    <script src="/js/jquery.min.js"></script>
    <script src="/js/bootstrap.min.js"></script>

  </body>
</html>
```

This template loads the CSS and scripts and contains the placeholders for the messages and main section.

We also need a small module that gets the main content and some other options and applies them to this template. We'll place it inside `templates/layout.js`:

```
var Plates = require('plates'),
    fs      = require('fs');

var templates = {
  layout : fs.readFileSync(__dirname + '/layout.html', 'utf8'),
  alert  : fs.readFileSync(__dirname + '/alert.html', 'utf8')
};

module.exports = function(main, title, options) {

  if (! options) {
    options = {};
  }

  var data = {
    "main-body": main,
    "title": title,
    'messages': ''
  };

  ['error', 'info'].forEach(function(messageType) {
    if (options[messageType]) {
      data.messages += Plates.bind(templates.alert,
        {message: options[messageType]});
    }
  });

  return Plates.bind(templates.layout, data);

};
```

In Node.js, a module is simply a JavaScript file that is intended to be used by other modules. All the variables inside a module are private; if the module author wishes to expose a value or a function to the outside world, it modifies or sets the special variable in `module.exports`.

In our case, this module exports a function that gets the markup for the main page content, the page title, and some options such as the info or the error message and applies it to the layout template.

We also need to place the following markup file under `templates/alert.html`:

```
<div class="alert">
  <a class="close" data-dismiss="alert">x</a>
  <p class="message"></p>
</div>
```

Now we're ready to start implementing some of the requirements.

User registration

This app will be offering users a personal to-do list. Before they can access it, they need to be signed up in the system. For that you need to define some URLs that the user will use to fetch our user sign-up form and submit it.

Now you will be changing the `app.js` file. This file contains a set of initialization procedures, including this block:

```
app.router.get('/', function () {
  this.res.json({ 'hello': 'world' })
});
```

This block is routing all the HTTP requests having a / URL and where the HTTP method is GET to the given function. This function will then be invoked for every request with these two characteristics in which case you are replying, `{"hello":"world"}`, which the user will see printed on the browser.

Now we need to remove this routing and add some routes that allow a user to register himself.

For that, create a folder named `routes` where you will place all the routing modules. The first one is `routes/users.js` and will contain the following code:

```
var fs      = require('fs'),
    couchdb = require('../lib/couchdb'),
    dbName  = 'users',
    db      = couchdb.use(dbName),
    Plates  = require('plates'),
    layout  = require('../templates/layout');

var templates = {
  'new' : fs.readFileSync(__dirname +
    '/../templates/users/new.html', 'utf8'),
  'show': fs.readFileSync(__dirname +
    '/../templates/users/show.html', 'utf8')
```

```
};

function insert(doc, key, callback) {
  var tried = 0, lastError;

  (function doInsert() {
    tried ++;
    if (tried >= 2) {
      return callback(lastError);
    }

    db.insert(doc, key, function(err) {
      if (err) {
        lastError = err;
        if (err.status_code === 404) {
          couchdb.db.create(dbName, function(err) {
            if (err) {
              return callback(err);
            }
            doInsert();
          });
        } else {
          return callback(err);
        }
      }
      callback.apply({}, arguments);
    });
  }());
}

function render(user) {
  var map = Plates.Map();
  map.where('id').is('email').use('email').as('value');
  map.where('id').is('password').use('password').as('value');
  return Plates.bind(templates['new'], user || {}, map);
}

module.exports = function() {
  this.get('/new', function() {
    this.res.writeHead(200, {'Content-Type': 'text/html'});
    this.res.end(layout(render(), 'New User'));
  });
```

```
    this.post('/', function() {

      var res = this.res,
          user = this.req.body;

      if (! user.email || ! user.password) {
        return this.res.end(layout(templates['new'],
          'New User', {error: 'Incomplete User Data'}));
      }

      insert(user, this.req.body.email, function(err) {
        if (err) {
          if (err.status_code === 409) {
            return res.end(layout(render(user), 'New User', {
              error: 'We already have a user with that email
address.'}));
          }
          console.error(err.trace);
          res.writeHead(500, {'Content-Type': 'text/html'});
          return res.end(err.message);
        }
        res.writeHead(200, {'Content-Type': 'text/html'});
        res.end(layout(templates['show'], 'Registration Complete'));
      });
    });

  };
```

This new module exports a function that will bind two new routes GET /new and
POST /. These routes will later be appended to the /users namespace, which means
that they will get activated when the server receives a GET request to /users/new
and a POST request to /users.

On the GET /new route, we will present a template that contains a user form. Place
it under templates/users/new.html:

```
<h1>New User</h1>
<form action="/users" method="POST">
  <p>
    <label for="email">E-mail</label>
    <input type="email" name="email" value="" id="email" />
  </p>
  <p>
    <label for="password">Password</label>
```

```
    <input type="password" name="password" id="password" value=""
required/>
  </p>
  <input type="submit" value="Submit" />
</form>
```

We will also need to create a `Thank you for registering` template, which you
need to place in `templates/users/show.html`:

```
<h1>Thank you!</h1>
<p>Thank you for registering. You can now <a href="/session/new">log
in here</a></p>
```

In the POST `/` route handler, we'll do some simple validation and insert the user
document into the CouchDB database by calling the function named `insert`. This
function tries to insert the user document and makes use of some clever error
handling. If the error is a "404 Not Found", it means that the `users` database hasn't
been created, and we take the opportunity to create it and automatically repeat
the user document insertion.

You're also catching the 409 Conflict HTTP status code, which CouchDB will return if
we try to insert a document with a key that already exists. Since we're using the user
e-mail as the document key, we inform the user that such a username already exists.

> Here, among other simplifications, you're storing the user password
> in plain text inside the database. This is obviously not recommended,
> but since the core of this book is not how to create a web application,
> this implementation detail is not relevant to your goals.

Now we need to attach these new routes to the `/users/` URL namespace by
updating and adding a line right before `app.start(3000)` in the file `app.js`:

```
var flatiron = require('flatiron'),
    path = require('path'),
    nstatic = require('node-static'),
    app = flatiron.app;

app.config.file({ file: path.join(__dirname, 'config', 'config.json')
});

var file = new nstatic.Server(__dirname + '/public/');
```

```
app.use(flatiron.plugins.http, {
  before: [
    function(req, res) {
      var found = app.router.dispatch(req, res);
      if (! found) {
        file.serve(req, res);
      }
    }
  ]
});

app.router.path('/users', require('./routes/users'));

app.start(3000);
```

Now you can start your application by typing in the command line:

```
$ node app
```

This starts the server. Then open a web browser and hit
`http://localhost:3000/users/new`. You will get a user form:

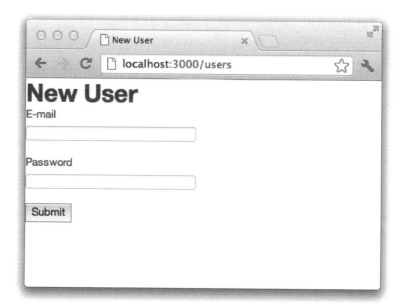

Submit an e-mail and a password and you will get a confirmation screen:

This screen will present you with a link to the /session/new URL, which doesn't exist yet.

Now you're ready to implement the login screens.

Logging in and session management

To be able to keep a session, your HTTP server needs to be able to do two things: parse cookies and store session data. For this we use two modules, namely, flatware-cookie-parser and flatware-session, which you should add to the package.json manifest:

```
{
  "description": "To-do App",
  "version": "0.0.0",
  "private": true,
  "dependencies": {
    "union": "0.3.0",
    "flatiron": "0.2.8",
    "plates": "0.4.x",
    "node-static": "0.6.0",
    "nano": "3.3.0",
    "flatware-cookie-parser": "0.1.x",
    "flatware-session": "0.1.x"
  },
  "scripts": {
    "test": "vows --spec",
```

```
      "start": "node app.js"
    },
    "name": "todo",
    "author": "Pedro",
    "homepage": ""
  }
```

Now, install the missing dependencies:

```
$ npm install
flatware-cookie-parser@0.1.0 node_modules/flatware-cookie-parser


flatware-session@0.1.0 node_modules/flatware-session
```

Next, add these middleware components to your server in the file app.js:

```
var flatiron = require('flatiron'),
    path = require('path'),
    nstatic = require('node-static'),
    app = flatiron.app;

app.config.file({ file: path.join(__dirname, 'config', 'config.json')
});

var file = new nstatic.Server(__dirname + '/public/');

app.use(flatiron.plugins.http, {
  before: [
    require('flatware-cookie-parser')(),
    require('flatware-session')(),
    function(req, res) {
      var found = app.router.dispatch(req, res);
      if (! found) {
        file.serve(req, res);
      }
    }
  ]
});

app.router.path('/users', require('./routes/users'));
app.router.path('/session', require('./routes/session'));
```

```
    app.start(3000);
```

We also need to create a `routes/session.js` module to handle the new session routes:

```
var plates  = require('plates'),
    fs      = require('fs'),
    couchdb = require('../lib/couchdb'),
    dbName  = 'users',
    db      = couchdb.use(dbName),
    Plates  = require('plates'),
    layout  = require('../templates/layout');

var templates = {
  'new' : fs.readFileSync(__dirname +
    '/../templates/session/new.html', 'utf8')
};

module.exports = function() {

  this.get('/new', function() {
    this.res.writeHead(200, {'Content-Type': 'text/html'});
    this.res.end(layout(templates['new'], 'Log In'));
  });

  this.post('/', function() {

    var res   = this.res,
        req   = this.req,
        login = this.req.body;

    if (! login.email || ! login.password) {
      return res.end(layout(templates['new'], 'Log In',
        {error: 'Incomplete Login Data'}));
    }

    db.get(login.email, function(err, user) {
      if (err) {
        if (err.status_code === 404) {
          // User was not found
          return res.end(layout(templates['new'], 'Log In',
            {error: 'No such user'}));
        }
```

```
        console.error(err.trace);
        res.writeHead(500, {'Content-Type': 'text/html'});
        return res.end(err.message);
      }

      if (user.password !== login.password) {
        res.writeHead(403, {'Content-Type': 'text/html'});
        return res.end(layout(templates['new'], 'Log In',
            {error: 'Invalid password'}));
      }

      // store session
      req.session.user = user;

      // redirect user to TODO list
      res.writeHead(302, {Location: '/todos'});
      res.end();
    });

  });

};
```

Next we need to add a view template under `templates/session/new.html` that contains the login form:

```html
<h1>Log in</h1>
<form action="/session" method="POST">
  <p>
    <label for="email">E-mail</label>
    <input type="email" name="email" value="" id="email"/>
  </p>
  <p>
    <label for="password">Password</label>
    <input type="password" name="password" id="password" value=""
required/>
  </p>
  <input type="submit" value="Log In" />
</form>
```

Next, stop the server if it's still running (by pressing *Ctrl + C*) and start it again:

```
$ node app.js
```

Point your browser to `http://localhost:3000/session/new` and insert the e-mail and password of a user you already have registered:

If the login succeeds, you will be redirected to the `/todos` URL, which the server does not respond to yet.

Next we're going to make the to-do list work.

The to-do list

For displaying the to-do list, we're going to use a table. It would be nice to sort the to-do items by using drag-and-drop. An easy way to enable this is by using jQuery UI. For this feature alone you don't need the full jQuery UI library, you can download a custom-built one by pointing your browser to `http://jqueryui.com/download`, deselecting every option except the **Sortable** option in the **Interactions** element, and clicking on the **Download** button. Unzip the resulting file and copy the `jquery-ui-1.8.23.custom.min.js` file into `public/js`.

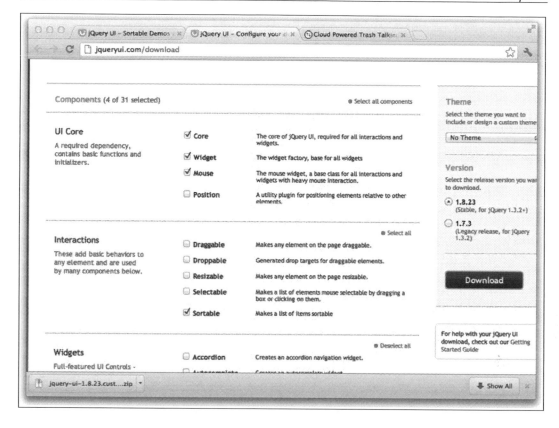

We need to refer this script in the `templates.html` or `layout.html` file:

```html
<html>
  <head>
    <meta http-equiv="Content-Type" content="text/html; charset=utf-8"
/>
    <title id="title"></title>
    <link href="/css/bootstrap.min.css" rel="stylesheet" />
  </head>
  <body>

    <section role="main" class="container">

      <div id="messages"></div>
```

```
        <div id="main-body"></div>

    </section>

    <script src="/js/jquery.min.js"></script>
    <script src="/js/jquery-ui-1.8.23.custom.min.js"></script>
    <script src="/js/bootstrap.min.js"></script>
    <script src="/js/todos.js"></script>
  </body>
</html>
```

You should also add a file under `public/js/todos.js` that will contain some frontend interactive code.

Now we need to respond to the `/todos` URL by firstly including the new routing in the `app.js` file:

```
var flatiron = require('flatiron'),
    path = require('path'),
    nstatic = require('node-static'),
    app = flatiron.app;

app.config.file({ file: path.join(__dirname, 'config', 'config.json')
});

var file = new nstatic.Server(__dirname + '/public/');

app.use(flatiron.plugins.http, {
  before: [
    require('flatware-cookie-parser')(),
    require('flatware-session')(),
    function(req, res) {
      var found = app.router.dispatch(req, res);
      if (! found) {
        file.serve(req, res);
      }
    }
  ]
});

app.router.path('/users', require('./routes/users'));
app.router.path('/session', require('./routes/session'));
app.router.path('/todos', require('./routes/todos'));

app.start(3000);
```

Then we need to place the new to-do routes module under `routes/todos.js`:

```
var fs      = require('fs'),
    couchdb = require('../lib/couchdb'),
    dbName  = 'todos',
    db      = couchdb.use(dbName),
    Plates  = require('plates'),
    layout  = require('../templates/layout'),
    loggedIn = require('../middleware/logged_in')();

var templates = {
  index : fs.readFileSync(__dirname +
    '/../templates/todos/index.html', 'utf8'),
  'new' : fs.readFileSync(__dirname +
    '/../templates/todos/new.html', 'utf8')
};

function insert(email, todo, callback) {
  var tries = 0,
      lastError;

  (function doInsert() {
    tries ++;
    if (tries >= 3) return callback(lastError);

    db.get(email, function(err, todos) {
      if (err && err.status_code !== 404) return callback(err);

      if (! todos) todos = {todos: []};
      todos.todos.unshift(todo);

      db.insert(todos, email, function(err) {
        if (err) {
          if (err.status_code === 404) {
            lastError = err;
            // database does not exist, need to create it
            couchdb.db.create(dbName, function(err) {
              if (err) {
                return callback(err);
              }
              doInsert();
            });
            return;
          }
```

```
            return callback(err);
        }
        return callback();
      });
    });
  })();

}

module.exports = function() {

  this.get('/', [loggedIn, function() {

    var res = this.res;

    db.get(this.req.session.user.email, function(err, todos) {

      if (err && err.status_code !== 404) {
        res.writeHead(500);
        return res.end(err.stack);
      }

      if (! todos) todos = {todos: []};
      todos = todos.todos;

      todos.forEach(function(todo, idx) {
        if (todo) todo.pos = idx + 1;
      });

      var map = Plates.Map();
      map.className('todo').to('todo');
      map.className('pos').to('pos');
      map.className('what').to('what');
      map.where('name').is('pos').use('pos').as('value');

      var main = Plates.bind(templates.index, {todo: todos}, map);
      res.writeHead(200, {'Content-Type': 'text/html'});
      res.end(layout(main, 'To-Dos'));

    });

  }]);
```

```
this.get('/new', [loggedIn, function() {

  this.res.writeHead(200, {'Content-Type': 'text/html'});
  this.res.end(layout(templates['new'], 'New To-Do'));
}]);


this.post('/', [loggedIn, function() {

  var req  = this.req,
      res  = this.res,
      todo = this.req.body
  ;

  if (! todo.what) {
    res.writeHead(200, {'Content-Type': 'text/html'});
    return res.end(layout(templates['new'], 'New To-Do',
      {error: 'Please fill in the To-Do description'}));
  }

  todo.created_at = Date.now();

  insert(req.session.user.email, todo, function(err) {

    if (err) {
      res.writeHead(500);
      return res.end(err.stack);
    }

    res.writeHead(303, {Location: '/todos'});
    res.end();
  });

}]);


this.post('/sort', [loggedIn, function() {

  var res = this.res,
      order = this.req.body.order && this.req.body.order.split(','),
      newOrder = []
      ;

  db.get(this.req.session.user.email, function(err, todosDoc) {
```

```
    if (err) {
      res.writeHead(500);
      return res.end(err.stack);
    }

    var todos = todosDoc.todos;

    if (order.length !== todos.length) {
      res.writeHead(409);
      return res.end('Conflict');
    }

    order.forEach(function(order) {
      newOrder.push(todos[parseInt(order, 10) - 1]);
    });

    todosDoc.todos = newOrder;

    db.insert(todosDoc, function(err) {
      if (err) {
        res.writeHead(500);
        return res.end(err.stack);
      }
      res.writeHead(200);
      res.end();
    });

  });
}]);


this.post('/delete', [loggedIn, function() {

  var req = this.req,
      res = this.res,
      pos = parseInt(req.body.pos, 10)
      ;

  db.get(this.req.session.user.email, function(err, todosDoc) {
    if (err) {
      res.writeHead(500);
      return res.end(err.stack);
    }
```

```
      var todos = todosDoc.todos;
      todosDoc.todos = todos.slice(0, pos - 1).concat(todos.
slice(pos));

      db.insert(todosDoc, function(err) {
        if (err) {
          res.writeHead(500);
          return res.end(err.stack);
        }
        res.writeHead(303, {Location: '/todos'});
        res.end();
      });

    });

  }]);

};
```

This module responds to the to-do index (GET /todos), fetching and presenting all the to-do items for the logged-in user. Place the following template under templates/todos/index.html:

```html
<h1>Your To-Dos</h1>

<a class="btn" href="/todos/new">New To-Do</a>

<table class="table">
  <thead>
    <tr>
      <th>#</th>
      <th>What</th>
      <th></th>
    </tr>
  </thead>
  <tbody id="todo-list">
    <tr class="todo">
      <td class="pos"></td>
      <td class="what"></td>
      <td class="remove">
        <form action="/todos/delete" method="POST">
          <input type="hidden" name="pos" value="" />
          <input type="submit" name="Delete" value="Delete" />
        </form>
      </td>
```

```
      </tr>
    </tbody>
  </table>
```

Another new route is GET /todos/new, presenting the user a form for creating a new to-do item. This route makes use of a new template placed in templates/todos/new.html:

```
<h1>New To-Do</h1>
<form action="/todos" method="POST">
  <p>
    <label for="email">What</label>
    <textarea name="what" id="what" required></textarea>
  </p>
  <input type="submit" value="Create" />
</form>
```

The POST /todos route creates a new to-do item by calling the local insert function, which handles the error for when the database does not exist, creating it as needed and retrying the insert function later.

The index template depends on the existence of a client-side script placed under public/js/todos.js:

```
$(function() {
  $('#todo-list').sortable({
    update: function() {
      var order = [];
      $('.todo').each(function(idx, row) {
        order.push($(row).find('.pos').text());
      });

      $.post('/todos/sort', {order: order.join(',')}, function() {
        $('.todo').each(function(idx, row) {
          $(row).find('.pos').text(idx + 1);
        });
      });

    }
  });
});
```

This file activates and handles the drag-and-drop item, making an AJAX call to the /todos/sort URL with the new order of the to-do items.

The **Delete** button on each item is also handled in the todos.js routing module by loading the user to-do items, removing the item at the given position and storing the items back.

 You may have noticed by now that we store all the to-do items for a given user inside one document in the todos database. This technique is simple and works well if all users keep the number of to-dos relatively low. Anyway, this detail is not important for our purpose.

To make this work, we need to provide a routing middleware under middleware/logged_in.js. This middleware component is responsible for protecting some routes and, when the user is not logged in, redirecting the user to the login screen instead of executing that route:

```
function LoggedIn() {
    return function(next) {
        if (! this.req.session || ! this.req.session.user) {
            this.res.writeHead(303, {Location: '/session/new'});
            return this.res.end();
        }
        next();
    };
}

module.exports = LoggedIn;
```

Finally, stop the server if it's still running (by hitting *Ctrl + C*) and start it up again:

```
$ node app.js
```

Point your browser to `http://localhost:3000/session/new`, and enter the e-mail and password of the user you already have registered. You will then be redirected to the to-do list of the user, which will start off empty.

You can now click on the **New To-Do** button, obtaining the following form:

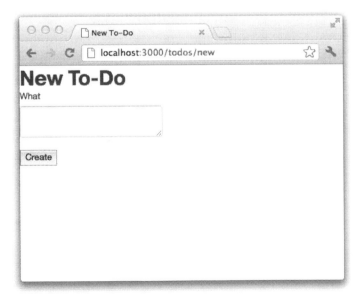

Insert some text and click on the **Create** button. The to-do item will be inserted in the database and the updated to-do list will be presented:

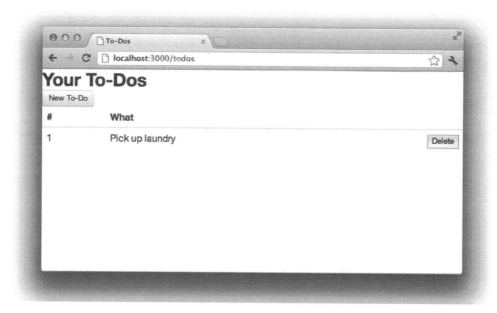

You can insert as many to-do items as you like. Once you've had enough, you can try to reorder them by dragging-and-dropping the table rows.

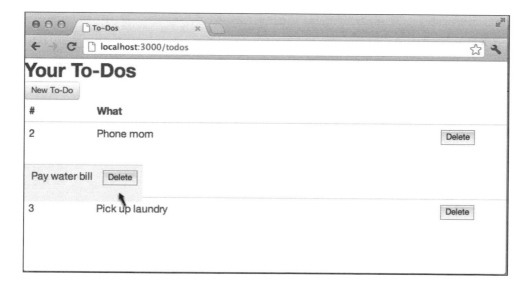

You can also click on the **Delete** button to remove a specific to-do item.

File summary

The following is a list of the files that compose this application:

```
$ tree
.
├── app.js
├── config
│   └── config.json
├── lib
│   └── couchdb.js
├── middleware
│   └── logged_in.js
├── package.json
├── public
│   ├── css
│   │   ├── bootstrap-responsive.css
│   │   ├── bootstrap-responsive.min.css
│   │   ├── bootstrap.css
│   │   └── bootstrap.min.css
│   ├── img
│   │   ├── glyphicons-halflings-white.png
│   │   └── glyphicons-halflings.png
│   └── js
│       ├── bootstrap.js
│       ├── bootstrap.min.js
│       ├── jquery-ui-1.8.23.custom.min.js
│       ├── jquery.min.js
│       └── todos.js
├── routes
│   ├── session.js
│   ├── todos.js
│   └── users.js
├── templates
│   ├── alert.html
│   ├── layout.html
│   ├── layout.js
```

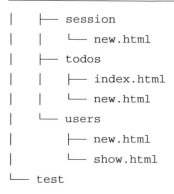

```
|     ├── session
|     |     └── new.html
|     ├── todos
|     |     ├── index.html
|     |     └── new.html
|     └── users
|           ├── new.html
|           └── show.html
└── test
```

13 directories, 27 files

Summary

In this chapter you learned how to create a simple web application using Node.js, Flatiron.js, and some other components.

This application will be the target of our user-interface tests in future chapters.

3
Installing Zombie.js and Mocha

By the end of this chapter you should be able to setup the base structure of a test environment for an application using Zombie.js and Mocha.

Topics covered in this chapter are:

- Setting up the Zombie.js and Mocha packages in your application manifest
- Setting up a test environment
- Running your first test

Changing the application manifest

You'll now be extending the to-do application you started building in the previous chapter and start providing it with the ability to test itself.

In the root of the application, you have a file named `package.json` that you already changed to introduce some modules that your application depends on. Now you need to add a new section that specifies the dependencies on other modules during the development and testing phase. This section is named `devDependencies` and is only installed by NPM if the NODE_ENV environment variable is not set to `production`. This is a good place to introduce the dependencies on modules that need to be there for running your tests.

First you need to add the mocha and zombie modules:

```
{
  "description": "To-do App",
  "version": "0.0.0",
  "private": true,
  "dependencies": {
    "union": "0.3.0",
    "flatiron": "0.2.8",
    "plates": "0.4.x",
    "node-static": "0.6.0",
    "nano": "3.3.0",
    "flatware-cookie-parser": "0.1.x",
    "flatware-session": "0.1.x"
  },
  "devDependencies": {
    "mocha": "1.4.x",
    "zombie": "1.4.x"
  },
  "scripts": {
    "test": "vows --spec",
    "start": "node app.js"
  },
  "name": "todo",
  "author": "Pedro",
  "homepage": ""
}
```

Then you will need to install these missing dependencies using NPM:

```
$ npm install
...
mocha@1.4.2 node_modules/mocha
...


zombie@1.4.1 node_modules/zombie
...
```

This will install these two modules and their internal dependencies inside the node_modules folder, making them available for your application at any time.

Setting up a test environment

You now need to set up a testing script. First you're going to test the user signup process.

But before that, in order for us to be able to start up our server from within the tests, we need to make a slight modification to the app.js file:

```
var flatiron = require('flatiron'),
    path = require('path'),
    nstatic = require('node-static'),
    app = flatiron.app;

app.config.file({ file: path.join(__dirname, 'config', 'config.json')
});

var file = new nstatic.Server(__dirname + '/public/');

app.use(flatiron.plugins.http, {
  before: [
    require('flatware-method-override')(),
    require('flatware-cookie-parser')(),
    require('flatware-session')(),
    function(req, res) {
      var found = app.router.dispatch(req, res);
      if (! found) {
        file.serve(req, res);
      }
    }
  ]
});

app.router.path('/users', require('./routes/users'));
app.router.path('/session', require('./routes/session'));
app.router.path('/todos', require('./routes/todos'));

module.exports = app;

if (process.mainModule === module) {
  app.start(3000);
}
```

Our tests will be using their own server, so we don't need app.js to run a server for us in this case. These last few lines export the application and only start up the server if the main module (the module that the node command line is called with) is the app.js one. Since the tests will have a different main module, the server won't start when we run the tests.

Now, as the first example, we're going to test the fetching of the user signup form. We're going to concentrate all the tests that are related to the user routes in a file under test/users.js. This file can start out with:

```
var assert  = require('assert'),
    Browser = require('zombie'),
    app     = require('../app')
    ;


before(function(done) {
  app.start(3000, done);
});


after(function(done) {
  app.server.close(done);
});


describe('Users', function() {

  describe('Signup Form', function() {

    it('should load the signup form', function(done) {
      var browser = new Browser();
      browser.visit("http://localhost:3000/users/new", function() {
        assert.ok(browser.success, 'page loaded');
        done();
      });
    });

  });

});
```

In the previous code, at the top, we include the assert module (used for verifying whether the app behaves as expected), the zombie module (assigned to the Browser variable), and the app module. The app module gets hold of the Flatiron application object so you can start and stop the corresponding server.

Next we declare that, before any test is run, the app should be started, and that after all the tests are done, the server should be closed.

Next up is a series of nested `describe` calls. These calls serve to give context to each test, allowing you to, later, differentiate the setup and teardown functions that will occur before and after each of the tests.

Then comes an `it` statement where you implement the test. This statement takes two arguments, namely, the description of what is being tested on the described subject and a function that will be called when the test is started. This function gets a callback function, `done` that is called on completion of the test. This arrangement makes asynchronous testing possible and reliable. Each test only ends when the respective `done` function is called, which can be after a series of asynchronous I/O calls.

Then we set out to create a browser and load the user signup form URL, using the `assert.ok` function to verify whether the page loads successfully. The `assert` module is a Node.js core module that provides basic assertion testing. Within the test code, we place some assertions to validate that some values are what we expect them to be. If any of the assertions fail, `assert` will throw an error, which will be caught by the test runner, signaling that the test has failed.

Besides the basic `assert.ok` function, which will throw an error if the value is not true (that is, passes the `x == true` test), this module also provides a set of helper functions to provide more elaborate comparisons such as `assert.deepEqual` and others. For more information about the `assert` module you can read the API documents at `http://nodejs.org/api/assert.html`.

Now we need to specify a test command script by replacing the default that Flatiron provided in `package.json`:

```
"scripts": {
  "test": "mocha test/users.js",
  "start": "node app.js"
},...
```

This specifies what NPM should do when told to run the tests. To run the tests enter the following command on the command line:

```
$ npm test
```

The output should be successful:

```
...
> mocha test/users.js

  .

  ✔ 1 test complete (284ms)
```

Summary

To install Mocha and Zombie, you need to include them as development dependencies in your application manifest and then use NPM to install them.

Once these modules are installed, you can create test files for each logical component of your application inside a directory named `test`. Each of these files should contain a series of tests, each of them properly contextualized inside nested `describe` statements.

You should also alter the application manifest to specify the testing script so that the tests are runnable using NPM.

In the following chapters, we'll be evolving this test and introduce some more, in order to cover more use cases of our application.

4
Understanding Mocha

In the previous chapter, we installed and introduced Mocha. Mocha is a JavaScript test framework that runs inside Node.js or inside a browser. You can use it to define and run your own tests. Mocha reports back on the outcome: which tests ran fine and which tests failed and where any failures occurred. Mocha runs each of the tests in turn, waiting for one test to finish or timeout before running the next one.

Even though Mocha is designed to be able to run on any modern browser, we will only be running it through Node.js via the command line. There are other things Mocha can do, which will be explained in this chapter. For a more complete reference to Mocha's capabilities, please visit Mocha's official documentation website, `http://visionmedia.github.com/mocha/` to find out more.

The topics covered in this chapter include:

- Describing features and using assertions
- Understanding how Mocha performs asynchronous tests

By the end of this chapter, you should be able to use Mocha to perform asynchronous tests and understand how Mocha controls test flow.

Organizing your tests

There are two strategies you can use to organize your tests. The first is to divide them somehow into separate files, each file representing a functional or logical unit of your application. The other strategy, which can be used in tandem with the first one, is to group them by feature.

Having a separate file for each functional unit of your app is a good way of separating your testing concerns. You should analyze the structure of your application and separate it into distinct concerns that have a minimum amount of overlap. For instance, your application may have to deal with user registrations— that could be one functional group. Another functional group may be user login. If your application deals with to-do lists, you may want to have a separate file that contains the tests for that part of your application.

By having separate files for each functional group, you can call your tests in isolation while you're working on that particular group. This technique also allows you to keep the line count low on each file, which is helpful when you're navigating and maintaining your tests.

Describing features: When defining your tests, you can also group application functionality by feature. For instance, when describing the to-do list functionality, you could further separate these features as follows:

- Creating a to-do item
- Removing a to-do item
- Showing the to-do list
- Changing the order of to-do list items

Within our test scripts, we would describe the previously mentioned testable to-do features.

The layout of the to-do items test file could then be as follows:

```
describe('To-do items', function() {

  describe('creating', function() {
    // to-do item creating tests here...
  });

  describe('removing', function() {
    // removing a to-do item tests here...
  });

  describe('showing', function() {
    // to-do item list showing tests here...
  });

  describe('ordering', function() {
    // to-do item ordering tests here...
  });

});
```

You can nest as many `describe` statements as you wish, refining the scope of the tests as much as you want, but as a rule of thumb, you should use two description levels: one for the functional group (for instance, to-do items) and another level for each feature. Inside each feature definition, you can place all the relevant tests.

Using before and after hooks

For any given group of tests, you can set certain pieces of code to run before or after all the tests. This can be useful for setting up databases, cleaning up some state after the tests, or generally, for setting up or tearing down some state that you need in order to run the test itself.

In this next example, the function named `runBefore` runs before any of the described tests:

```
describe('some feature', function() {

  before(function runBefore() {
    console.log('running before function...');  });

  it('should do A', function() {
    console.log('test A');
  });

  it('should do B', function() {
    console.log('test B');
  });
});
```

Save this file code into a file named `test.js` and install Mocha locally:

```
$ npm install mocha
```

Run the tests:

```
$ node_modules/.bin/mocha test.js
```

It should give you the following output:

```
  running before function...
test A
.test B
.

  ✔ 2 tests complete (6ms)
```

In a similar way, you can also specify a function to be executed after all the tests are done:

```
describe('some feature', function() {

  after(function runAfter() {
    console.log('running after function...');  });

  it('should do A', function() {
    console.log('test A');
  });

  it('should do B', function() {
    console.log('test B');
  });
});
```

Running this code produces the following output, as you might expect:

```
  test A
.test B
.running after function...

  ✔ 2 tests complete (6ms)
```

A function can also be defined to be called before (or after) each and every test in the block, using the beforeEach and afterEach keywords respectively. Sample usage of the beforeEach keyword is as follows:

```
describe('some feature', function() {

  beforeEach(function runBeforeEach() {
    console.log('running beforeEach function...');  });
```

```
  it('should do A', function() {
    console.log('test A');
  });

  it('should do B', function() {
    console.log('test B');
  });
});
```

If you run this test, the output will be:

```
  running beforeEach function...
test A
.running beforeEach function...
test B

.
```

✔ 2 tests complete (6ms)

Naturally, the `afterEach` code calls the function after each test is performed.

Using asynchronous hooks

Any of these functions that you run before any or all your tests can be asynchronous.
If a function is asynchronous, simply accept a callback argument like this one:

```
describe('some feature', function() {
  function runBeforeEach(done) {
    console.log('running afterEach function...');
    setTimeout(done, 1000);
  }
  beforeEach(runBeforeEach);

  it('should do A', function() {
    console.log('test A');
  });

  it('should do B', function() {
    console.log('test B');
  });
});
```

When running this test code, you will notice the one-second lag before running each test, which—had we not provided the callback argument—would not have been observed.

How hooks interact with test groups

As we've seen, inside a describe scope, you can have respective before, after, beforeEach, and afterEach hooks. If you have a nested describe scope, that scope can also have hooks. In addition to the hooks on the current scope, Mocha will also call the hooks on all the parent scopes. Consider this code where we declare a two-level nesting:

```
describe('feature A', function() {

  before(function() {
    console.log('before A');
  });

  after(function() {
    console.log('after A');
  });

  beforeEach(function() {
    console.log('beforeEach A');
  });

  afterEach(function() {
    console.log('afterEach A');
  });

  describe('feature A.1', function() {
    before(function() {
      console.log('before A.1');
    });

    after(function() {
      console.log('after A.1');
    });

    beforeEach(function() {
      console.log('beforeEach A.1');
    });
```

```
    afterEach(function() {
      console.log('afterEach A.1');
    });

    it('should do A.1.1', function() {
      console.log('A.1.1');
    });

    it('should do A.1.2', function() {
      console.log('A.1.2');
    });

  });

});
```

When running the preceding code, the output is:

```
  before A
before A.1
beforeEach A
beforeEach A.1
A.1.1
.afterEach A.1
afterEach A
beforeEach A
beforeEach A.1
A.1.2
.afterEach A.1
afterEach A
after A.1
after A


  ✔ 4 tests complete (16ms)
```

Using assertions

Now that you have a place for testing your code, you need some way of verifying that your code runs as expected. For this, you need an assertion testing library.

There are many assertion testing libraries for many programming styles, but here we're going to use the one that already comes bundled with Node.js, the `assert` module. It contains the smallest set of utility functions you need to describe what expectations you have for each test. At the top of each testing file, you need the assertion library using `require`:

```
var assert = require('assert');
```

> You can assert the "truthiness" of any expression. "Truthy" and "falsy" are concepts in JavaScript (and other languages), where type coercion allows certain values to equate to Boolean true or false, respectively. Some examples are as follows:
>
> ```
> var a = true;
> assert.ok(a, 'a should be truthy');
> ```
>
> The falsy values are:
> - `false`
> - `null`
> - `undefined`
> - the empty string
> - `0` (the number zero)
> - `NaN`
>
> All other values are truthy.

You can also test for equality using `assert.equal`:

```
var a = 'ABC';
assert.equal(a, 'ABC');
```

You can also conversely test for inequality using `assert.notEqual`:

```
var a = 'ABC';
assert.notEqual(a, 'ABCDEF');
```

These last two tests are equivalent to the JavaScript `==` (loose equals) operator, which means that they work for Booleans, strings, `undefined`, and `null` but fail for objects and arrays. For instance, this assertion will fail:

```
assert.equal({a:1}, {a:1});
```

It will fail because, in JavaScript, there is no native way to compare the equivalence of two objects rendering the following expression false:

```
{a: 1} == {a:1}
```

To compare objects (including arrays), you should use `assert.deepEqual`:

```
assert.deepEqual({a:1}, {a:1});
assert.deepEqual([0,1], [0,1]);
```

This function recurses through both comparing objects to find whether they somehow differ. This function also works, as the name implies, for deeply nested objects:

```
assert.deepEqual({a:[0,1], b: {c:2}}, {a:[0,1], b: {c:2}});
```

You can also test for deep inequality:

```
assert.notDeepEqual({a:[0,1], b: {c:2}}, {a:[0,1], b: {c:2, d: 3}});
```

Changing the assertion message

When an assertion fails, an error is thrown containing a message where both the expected and the actual values are printed:

```
> var a = false;
> assert.ok(a)
AssertionError: false == true
    at repl:1:9
    at REPLServer.self.eval (repl.js:111:21)
    at Interface.<anonymous> (repl.js:250:12)
    at Interface.EventEmitter.emit (events.js:88:17)
    at Interface._onLine (readline.js:199:10)
    at Interface._line (readline.js:517:8)
    at Interface._ttyWrite (readline.js:735:14)
    at ReadStream.onkeypress (readline.js:98:10)
    at ReadStream.EventEmitter.emit (events.js:115:20)
    at emitKey (readline.js:1057:12)
```

If you wish, you can replace this default message type with another, more contextualized one. This is achieved by passing in the message as the last argument for any of the assertion functions:

```
var result = 'ABC';
assert.equal(result, 'DEF', 'the result of operation X should be
DEF');
```

Performing asynchronous tests

Mocha runs all the tests in series, where each test can be synchronous or asynchronous. For a synchronous test, the test callback function should not accept any argument, as in the previous examples. But since Node.js doesn't block I/O operations, and we need to perform I/O operations for each of our tests (making at least an HTTP request to our server), our tests need to be asynchronous.

To make a test asynchronous, the test function should accept a callback function such as this:

```
it('tests something asynchronous', function(done) {
  doSomethingAsynchronous(function(err) {
    assert.ok(! err);
    done();
  });
});
```

The done callback function also accepts an error as the first argument, which means that instead of throwing an error, you can just call done directly:

```
it('tests something asynchronous', function(done) {
  doSomethingAsynchronous(function(err) {
    done(err);
  });
});
```

If you don't need to test the asynchronous function return value, you can pass the done function directly, like this:

```
it('tests something asynchronous', function(done) {
  doSomethingAsynchronous(done);
});
```

Timeouts: By default, Mocha reserves 2 seconds for each asynchronous test. You can change that globally by passing in the -t argument to Mocha:

```
$ node_modules/.bin/mocha test.js -t 4s
```

Here, you can use the number of seconds suffixed by s, as shown, or you can simply pass the number of milliseconds:

```
$ node_modules/.bin/mocha test.js -t 4000
```

You can also specify the timeout on any test by using `this.timeout(ms)` like this:

```
it('tests something asynchronous', function(done) {
  this.timeout(500); // 500 milliseconds
  doSomethingAsynchronous(done);
});
```

Summary

Mocha is a framework that runs your tests. You should split your tests into several files according to the functional areas you want to cover, and then describe each feature and define the necessary tests for each feature.

For each of these test groups, you optionally specify callback to be invoked using `before`, `beforeEach`, `after`, and `afterEach`. These callbacks are where the setup and teardown functions are specified. Each of these teardown or setup functions can be either synchronous or asynchronous. Furthermore, each of the tests themselves can be made to function asynchronously simply by passing a callback to the test, which will be invoked once the test is complete.

For asynchronous tests, Mocha reserves a default timeout of 2 seconds that you can override globally or on a per-test basis.

In the following chapter we will see how you can start using Zombie.js to simulate and manipulate a browser.

5
Manipulating the Zombie Browser

Now that we have our to-do HTTP application and understand how the Mocha testing framework works, we are ready to start creating tests using Zombie.js.

As covered before, Zombie.js allows you to create a simulated browser environment and manipulate it. These manipulations are the usual things users do with browsers, such as visiting a URL, clicking on links, filling and submitting forms, and others.

This chapter covers the following:

- Visiting a URL
- Filling and submitting a form
- Checking for errors in the browser
- Validating document content
- Understanding CSS selector syntax

This chapter shows you how you can setup a Zombie.js browser that interacts with your web application.

Visiting a URL: First, we are going to pick up our application tests from where we left off. The whole app concerns users, but in this part, we're mainly going to focus on functionality that the Users routes touch—rendering a signup form and actually creating a user record in the database.

As mentioned, we left off with this single test file:

```
var assert  = require('assert'),
    Browser = require('zombie'),
    app     = require('../app')
    ;


describe('Users', function() {

  before(function(done) {
    app.start(3000, done);
  });

  after(function(done) {
    app.server.close(done);
  });

  describe('Signup Form', function() {

    it('should load the signup form', function(done) {
      var browser = new Browser();
      browser.visit("http://localhost:3000/users/new", function() {
        assert.ok(browser.success, 'page loaded');
        done();
      });
    });

  });
});
```

This test simply loaded the user signup form and tested whether the browser considered it a success. Let's go through this test to fully understand what is going on.

First we create a new browser by instantiating a new browser object:

```
var browser = new Browser();
```

This creates a Zombie.js browser, which represents an independent browser process that has the main job of maintaining state across requests: the URL history, the cookies, and the local storage.

A browser also has a main window, and you can load a URL in it by using `browser.visit()`, like this:

```
browser.visit("http://localhost:3000/users/new");
```

This makes the browser perform an HTTP GET request to load the HTML page from that URL. Since Node.js and Zombie.js do asynchronous I/O processing, this only makes Zombie.js to start loading the page. Then Zombie.js tries to fetch the URL, parse the HTML document, and resolve all the dependencies by loading the referenced JavaScript files.

Once all that is done, we can be notified by passing a callback function to the `browser.wait()` method, like this:

```
browser.visit("http://localhost:3000/users/new");
browser.wait(function() {
  console.log('browser page loaded');
});
```

Instead of using the `browser.wait` function, we pass a callback directly into the `browser.visit()` call, like this:

```
browser.visit("http://localhost:3000/users/new",
  function(err, browser) {
    if (err) throw err;
    assert.ok(browser.success, 'page loaded');
    done();
  }
);
```

Here you pass in a callback function that gets invoked once there is an error or the browser is ready. If an error occurs, it is returned as the first argument—we check whether an error exists and throw it if it does, so that the test fails.

The second argument containing the browser object, which is the same as the browser object we already had. This means that we can omit the second argument altogether and work with the previous browser reference, like this:

```
browser.visit("http://localhost:3000/users/new",
  function(err) {
    if (err) throw err;
    assert.ok(browser.success, 'page loaded');
    done();
  }
);
```

If it's the same browser object, you may ask why that object is even passed. It's there to support this form of invocation:

```
var Browser = require('zombie');

Browser.visit(("http://localhost:3000/users/new",
  function(err, browser) {
    if (err) throw err;
    assert.ok(browser.success, 'page loaded');
    done();
  }
);
```

Note that here we're using the capitalized pseudo-class `Browser` object; we're not instantiating `browser`. Instead, we're leaving that up to the `Browser` module to do it and to pass it on to us as the second argument of our callback function.

 From now on, we will prefer this last succinct form to the others shown here.

When is the browser ready?

When we ask the browser to visit a URL, it calls us back when it's finished, but as web developers know, it's tricky to know exactly when a page load can be considered fully finished

A browser object has its own event loop that handles asynchronous events, such as loading resources, events, timeouts, and intervals. After a page is loaded and parsed, all the dependencies are loaded and parsed asynchronously—just like in real browsers—using this event loop.

Some of these dependencies may contain JavaScript files that will be loaded, parsed, and evaluated. Furthermore, the HTML document may contain some additional inline scripts that will be executed. If any of these scripts have a callback waiting for the document to be ready, these callbacks will be executed before your `browser.visit()` callback fires your test callback. This means that if, for instance, you have jQuery code that gets fired when the document is ready, it will run before your callback. The same can be said for any subsequent AJAX callbacks.

To see this in action, try adding the following code immediately before the closing `</body>` tag in the `templates/layout.html` file:

```
<script>
  $(function() {
    $.get('/users/new', function() {
      console.log('LOADED NEW');
    });
  });
</script>
```

Then change the test code in `test/users.js` so that it logs when the visit callback gets fired:

```
it('should load the signup form', function(done) {
  Browser.visit("http://localhost:3000/users/new", function(err,
browser) {
    if (err) throw err;
    console.log('VISIT IS DONE');
    assert.ok(browser.success, 'page loaded');
    done();
  });
});
```

To analyze this, we are going to run our tests in debug mode. In this mode, Zombie.js outputs some useful information, which includes the HTTP request activity that the browser is carrying out. To enable this mode, set the DEBUG environment variable like this:

```
$ DEBUG=true node_modules/.bin/mocha test/users.js
```

You should now get the following debug output:

```
Zombie: GET http://localhost:3000/users/new => 200

Zombie: GET http://localhost:3000/js/jquery.min.js => 200

Zombie: GET http://localhost:3000/js/jquery-ui-1.8.23.custom.min.js =>
200

Zombie: GET http://localhost:3000/js/bootstrap.min.js => 200

Zombie: GET http://localhost:3000/js/todos.js => 200

Zombie: GET http://localhost:3000/users/new => 200
```

```
LOADED NEW
VISIT IS DONE
.
```

```
✔ 1 test complete (315ms)
```

 If you are a Windows user, this last command will not work. You will need to set the DEBUG environment variable before running the Mocha command:

`$ SET DEBUG=true`

You will also need to replace the forward slashes (/) to backslashes (\):

`$ node_modules\.bin\mocha test\users.js`

As you can see, the LOADED NEW string is printed before the VISIT IS DONE string, which means that the browser performed and finished the AJAX request before your visit callback fired. You may wish to return to the code now and remove this extra console logging.

Options when visiting URLs

You can also pass in some options to the browser, to modify some of the actions and conditions regarding how it loads the page. These options come in the form of an object that you pass as an argument to the `Browser.visit()` call, right before the callback, like this:

```
Browser.visit(<url>, <options>, <callback>);
```

Here are the most useful options that we will discuss in detail:

- debug
- headers
- maxWait

debug

As we've seen, by setting the DEBUG environment variable, you can get some output from Zombie.js. This feature can also be activated by setting the debug option to `true`, like this:

```
Browser.visit(url, {debug: true}, callback);
```

headers

You can define a set of headers to be sent out on each HTTP request that originates from this visit. By default, Zombie.js sends these header values:

- **user-agent**: Mozilla/5.0, Chrome/10.0.613.0, Safari/534.15, or Zombie. js/1.4.1
- **accept-encoding**: identity
- **host**: localhost:3000
- **connection**: keep-alive

The `user-agent` header defines a fake user agent that somewhat mimics the Mozilla, Chrome, and Safari browsers, but you can change that in this setting, as you'll see later.

The `accept-encoding` header is specifying that no encoding should be done on the resulting document.

The `host` header is required as of HTTP 1.1 and specifies which hostname you're referring to for this request.

The `connection: keep-alive` header specifies that the connection to the server should be kept open after the request is done. This is an internal option that allows Node to reuse client-side sockets throughout many HTTP connections, which will slightly speed up your tests.

To add an additional header value, should your application need any, specify them like this:

```
var options = {
  headers: {
    'x-test': 'Test 123',
    'x-test-2': 'Test 234'
  }
};
Browser.visit(url, options, callback);
```

Note that these values will also be sent for every request when loading dependencies such as subsequent CSS and JavaScript files referred to in your HTML document.

maxWait

By default, when calling `Browser.visit`, Zombie.js loads the page, parses it, loads the dependencies, and runs any pending JavaScript code in the browser. If this takes more than 5 seconds, an error will be raised and your test will fail. If, for any reason, 5 seconds is not enough for all of this to happen, the limit can be increased by changing the `maxWait` option like this:

```
Browser.visit(url, {maxWait: '10s'}, callback);
```

You can specify the value as a string as `10ms`, `100ms`, `7.5s`, and so on..

Checking the existence of elements

When the `Browser.visit()` callback is fired, we check for errors. We also check whether the page was successfully loaded if the HTTP response status code was between 200 and 299. These 2XX response codes correspond to the `ok` request state and are part of the server's way of telling the user-agent that everything went well.

Despite receiving an `ok` response, we shouldn't take the server's word for granted. We may have received the response status code and an HTML document, but can't be sure that we got the intended document containing the markup for the user signup form.

In our case, we may wish to verify that the document has a heading element containing the `New User` string and that the new user form elements are present. Here is the code for the complete test:

```
it('should load the signup form', function(done) {
  Browser.visit("http://localhost:3000/users/new", function(err,
browser) {
    if (err) throw err;
    assert.ok(browser.success, 'page loaded');
    assert.equal(browser.text('h1'), 'New User');

    var form = browser.query('form');
    assert(form, 'form exists');
    assert.equal(form.method, 'POST', 'uses POST method');
    assert.equal(form.action, '/users', 'posts to /users');

    assert(browser.query('input[type=email]#email', form),
      'has email input');
    assert(browser.query('input[type=password]#password', form),
      'has password input');
```

```
    assert(browser.query('input[type=submit]', form),
      'has submit button');

  done();
  });
});
```

The new lines on the test are highlighted. Let's go through them now.

```
  assert.equal(browser.text('h1'), 'New User');
```

Here, `browser.text(<selector>)` is being used to extract the text content of the `h1` tag if (at least) one exists.

> If a selector matches more than one HTML element (which would happen if you had, in this case, more than one `h1` tag in the document), `browser.text(<selector>)` will return the concatenated text of all the matched nodes.

Here, the selector is just the tag name, but you can use any Sizzle-valid selector. These are similar to CSS3 selectors, which are also used in jQuery. If you're not familiar with these, don't worry, we will be seeing more examples of these in the future.

```
  var form = browser.query('form');
  assert(form, 'form exists');
```

> The browser (and all browsers) stores the representation of the current document in an accessible structure called **Document Object Module (DOM)**. The HTML markup inside a document is parsed by the browser and the DOM tree is built. This DOM can be traversed programmatically using JavaScript.

Here we are using the `browser.query(<selector>)` method to extract the first form element. This element is a DOM node, as you would find in the browser, and it respects the DOM specification. For now, we're only testing whether it exists. After this, we are going to check whether some attributes are correct:

```
  assert.equal(form.method, 'POST', 'uses POST method');
  assert.equal(form.action, '/users', 'posts to /users');
```

Here we're verifying that the form method is POST and that, when the user submits it, it actually posts to the /users URL.

Next we verify if the form elements that are necessary to create a user are present:

```
assert(browser.query('input[type=email]#email', form),
    'has email input');
assert(browser.query('input[type=password]#password', form),
    'has password input');
assert(browser.query('input[type=submit]', form),
    'has submit button');
```

We're using the `browser.query(<selector>, <context>)` form to retrieve the first matching node, but this time, we're restraining the search to the subset child of `<context>`, which in our case is our `form` node. We are also using more complex selectors here, combining the tag name selector (`form`) with the ID selector `#id` and the attribute selector `[type=email]`. For instance, the first selector, `input[type=email]#email`, selects inputs that have the attribute of type `email` and an ID of the value `email`. This way, we're asserting that such an element exists since, if it didn't exist, the `browser.query()` call would return `undefined`, breaking the assert call.

Filling a form

Once you have loaded a page containing the user subscription form, you can fill the form and submit it back to the server. For this, we will use a new test case:

```
it("should submit", function(done) {
  Browser.visit("http://localhost:3000/users/new", function(err,
browser) {
    if (err) throw err;

    browser
      .fill('E-mail', 'me@email.com')
      .fill('Password', 'mypassword')
      .pressButton('Submit', function(err) {
        if (err) throw err;
        assert.equal(browser.text('h1'), 'Thank you!');
        assert(browser.query('a[href="/session/new"]'),
          'has login link');
        done();
      });

  });
});
```

Here we're revisiting the user creation form, and once the form has loaded, we're filling in the e-mail and password fills by using the `browser.fill(<field>, <value>)` method. In this form, `browser.fill()` accepts several types of arguments as a field identifier. Here we're using the label text that precedes the field. If you view the source for the empty user creation form, it will be:

```
<form action="/users" method="POST">
  <p>
    <label for="email">E-mail</label>
    <input type="email" name="email" value="" id="email">
  </p>
  <p>
    <label for="password">Password</label>
    <input type="password" name="password" id="password" value=""
required="">
  </p>
  <input type="submit" value="Submit">
</form>
```

Each of the two label tags we are using here has a `for` attribute that indicates the `id` attribute of the tag it relates to. This is what Zombie.js uses to match the field in `browser.fill()`. Alternatively, we could also specify the field name or CSS selector, making the following fill directives equivalent to what we have:

```
browser
  .fill('#email', 'me@email.com')
  .fill('#password', 'mypassword')
```

You can then run the test by typing on the shell console:

```
$ ./node_modules/.bin/mocha test/users.js
```

Provided the CouchDB server is accessible, these tests should then pass:

```
  ..


✔ 2 tests complete (577ms)
```

But, if you run the tests again, they should fail. Try it now:

```
  ..


✖ 1 of 2 tests failed:
```

```
1) Users Signup Form should submit:
   Error: Server returned status code 409
```

. . .

This is because we don't allow two users with the same e-mail address, and the browser yields a 409 response code as the result of such a user creation request. You could remove the user document from the database by hand before each test, but to fully remedy this, we need to automate the process.

First we're going to introduce the concept of fixtures. This is where we will define the username and password for our user, which will be used in other tests. You then need to create a file under `test/fixtures.json` with the following data for now:

```json
{
  "user" : {
    "email": "me@email.com",
    "password": "mypassword"
  }
}
```

This JSON file will then be consumed by the `users` test file by placing `require` right at the top:

```
var fixtures = require('./fixtures');
```

Then you also need to access the database, and for doing that we use the same library that the route listeners use:

```
var couchdb = require('../lib/couchdb'),
    dbName  = 'users',
    db      = couchdb.use(dbName);
```

Now we need to add a before hook into the `Signup Form` test description scope:

```
before(function(done) {
  db.get(fixtures.user.email, function(err, doc) {
    if (err && err.status_code === 404) return done();
    if (err) throw err;
    db.destroy(doc._id, doc._rev, done);
  });
});
```

This will make sure there is no such user record in our database.

Now that we're using fixtures, let's remove those hard-coded username and password strings from our test code:

```
it("should submit", function(done) {

  Browser.visit("http://localhost:3000/users/new", function(err,
browser) {
    if (err) throw err;

    browser
      .fill('E-mail', fixtures.user.email)
      .fill('Password', fixtures.user.password)
      .pressButton('Submit', function(err) {
        if (err) throw err;
        assert.equal(browser.text('h1'), 'Thank you!');
        assert(browser.query('a[href="/session/new"]'),
          'has login link');
        done();
      });

  });
});
```

This would then be the whole assembled user test file:

```
var assert  = require('assert'),
    Browser = require('zombie'),
    app     = require('../app'),
    couchdb = require('../lib/couchdb'),
    dbName  = 'users',
    db      = couchdb.use(dbName),
    fixtures = require('./fixtures');

describe('Users', function() {

  before(function(done) {
    app.start(3000, done);
  });

  after(function(done) {
    app.server.close(done);
  });

  describe('Signup Form', function() {
```

```
    before(function(done) {
      db.get(fixtures.user.email, function(err, doc) {
        if (err && err.status_code === 404) return done();
        if (err) throw err;
        db.destroy(doc._id, doc._rev, done);
      });
    });


    it('should load the signup form', function(done) {
      Browser.visit("http://localhost:3000/users/new", function(err,
browser) {
        if (err) throw err;
        assert.ok(browser.success, 'page loaded');
        assert.equal(browser.text('h1'), 'New User');

        var form = browser.query('form');

        assert(form, 'form exists');
        assert.equal(form.method, 'POST', 'uses POST method');
        assert.equal(form.action, '/users', 'posts to /users');

        assert(browser.query('input[type=email]#email', form),
          'has email input');
        assert(browser.query('input[type=password]#password', form),
          'has password input');
        assert(browser.query('input[type=submit]', form),
          'has submit button');

        done();
      });
    });

    it("should submit", function(done) {

      Browser.visit("http://localhost:3000/users/new", function(err,
browser) {
        if (err) throw err;

        browser
          .fill('E-mail', fixtures.user.email)
          .fill('Password', fixtures.user.password)
          .pressButton('Submit', function(err) {
            if (err) throw err;
```

```
            assert.equal(browser.text('h1'), 'Thank you!');
            assert(browser.query('a[href="/session/new"]'),
              'has login link');
            done();
          });

        });
      });

    });
  });
```

When running this test repeatedly, you should always get a success message now.

Testing the login form

Now that we have the user creation flow tested, let's test if that user can log in.

Following the test file pattern we have been using, you need to create a file under `test/session.js` with the following content:

1. First, import the missing dependencies:

```
var assert  = require('assert'),
    Browser = require('zombie'),
    app     = require('../app'),
    couchdb = require('../lib/couchdb'),
    dbName  = 'users',
    db      = couchdb.use(dbName),
    fixtures = require('./fixtures');

describe('Session', function() {

  before(function(done) {
    app.start(3000, done);
  });

  after(function(done) {
    app.server.close(done);
  });
```

That concludes the opening ceremonies!

2. Now we are ready to start describing the login form:

```
describe('Log in form', function() {

  before(function(done) {
    db.get(fixtures.user.email, function(err, doc) {
      if (err && err.status_code === 404) {
        return db.insert(fixtures.user, fixtures.user.email,
done);
      }
      if (err) throw err;
      done();
    });
  });
```

This `before` hook creates the test user document if one doesn't exist (instead of removing if it existed).

3. Next, we will test whether the login form loads and contains the relevant elements:

```
it('should load', function(done) {
  Browser.visit("http://localhost:3000/session/new",
    function(err, browser) {
      if (err) throw err;
      assert.ok(browser.success, 'page loaded');
      assert.equal(browser.text('h1'), 'Log in');

      var form = browser.query('form');

      assert(form, 'form exists');
      assert.equal(form.method, 'POST', 'uses POST method');
      assert.equal(form.action, '/session', 'posts to /
session');

      assert(browser.query('input[type=email]#email', form),
        'has email input');
      assert(browser.query('input[type=password]#password',
form),
        'has password input');
      assert(browser.query('input[type=submit]', form),
        'has submit button');
```

```
          done();
        });
      });
```

The only difference here from the user code is that the heading string should be `Log in` instead of `New User`. This happens because we have such a minimal user creation form, which suits us for the time being.

4. Next we are testing to see whether the login form actually works:

```
it("should allow you to log in", function(done) {

  Browser.visit("http://localhost:3000/session/new",
    function(err, browser) {
      if (err) throw err;

      browser
        .fill('E-mail', fixtures.user.email)
        .fill('Password', fixtures.user.password)
        .pressButton('Log In', function(err) {
          if (err) throw err;

          assert.equal(browser.location.pathname, '/todos',
            'should be redirected to /todos');
          done();
        });

    });
  });
});
```

Here we're loading and filling in the e-mail and password fields and clicking on the **Log In** button. When clicking on the button, the login form is posted, the session is initiated, and the user is redirected to the to-do items page.

5. Now run this test file from the command line:

```
$ ./node_modules/.bin/mocha test/session.js

  ..


  ✔ 2 tests complete (750ms)
```

6. This test includes the case for when the user enters the right username and password, but what happens when that's not the case? Let's create a test case for it:

```
it("should not allow you to log in with wrong password",
function(done) {

  Browser.visit("http://localhost:3000/session/new",
    function(err, browser) {
      if (err) throw err;

    browser
      .fill('E-mail', fixtures.user.email)
      .fill('Password', fixtures.user.password +
        'thisisnotmypassword')
      .pressButton('Log In', function(err) {
        assert(err, 'expected an error');
        assert.equal(browser.statusCode, 403,
          'replied with 403 status code');
        assert.equal(browser.location.pathname, '/session');
        assert.equal(browser.text('#messages .alert .message'),
          'Invalid password');
        done();
      });
    }
  );
});
```

Here we're loading and filling the login form, but this time we're providing a wrong password. After clicking on the **Log In** button, the server should return 403 status code, which will trigger an error passed in to our callback. Then we need to check the return status code by inspecting the browser.statusCode attribute, making sure it's the expected 403 forbidden code. Then we also verify that the user did not get redirected to the /todo URL and that the response document contains an alert message saying Invalid password.

Testing the to-do list

Now that we're done with the user registration and the session initiation, we are ready to test the core of our app, which is to manage to-do items. We will start by segregating that part of the application tests into a file of their own at `test/todos.js`, which may start with the following boilerplate:

```
var assert   = require('assert'),
    Browser  = require('zombie'),
    app      = require('../app'),
    couchdb  = require('../lib/couchdb'),
    dbName   = 'todos',
    db       = couchdb.use(dbName),
    fixtures = require('./fixtures'),
    login    = require('./login');

describe('Todos', function() {

  before(function(done) {
    app.start(3000, done);
  });

  after(function(done) {
    app.server.close(done);
  });

  beforeEach(function(done) {
    db.get(fixtures.user.email, function(err, doc) {
      if (err && err.status_code === 404) return done();
      if (err) throw err;
      db.destroy(doc._id, doc._rev, done);
    });
  });
});
```

Here we have similar boilerplate code for the other modules, with the difference that now we are dealing with a database named `todos`, not `users`. Another difference is that we want to start with a clean to-do list for each test, so we're adding a `beforeEach` hook that removes all the to-do items for the test user.

We are now ready to start carving out some tests, but there is at least one cumbersome repetitive task ahead that can be avoided at an early stage: logging in. We should assume that each test is individually reproducible and that the ordering of the tests doesn't matter—each test should rely on one browser instance, mimicking one individual user session per test. Also, since all the to-do item manipulation is scoped to a user and the user session must be initiated, we need to abstract that away into its own module inside `test/login.js`:

```
var Browser = require('zombie'),
    fixtures = require('./fixtures'),
    assert = require('assert'),
    couchdb = require('../lib/couchdb'),
    dbName = 'users',
    db     = couchdb.use(dbName);


function ensureUserExists(next) {
  db.get(fixtures.user.email, function(err, user) {
    if (err && err.status_code === 404) {
      db.insert(fixtures.user, fixtures.user.email, next);
    }
    if (err) throw err;
    next();
  });
}


module.exports = function(next) {
  return function(done) {

    ensureUserExists(function(err) {
      if (err) throw err;
      Browser.visit("http://localhost:3000/session/new",
        function(err, browser) {
          if (err) throw err;

          browser
            .fill('E-mail', fixtures.user.email)
            .fill('Password', fixtures.user.password)
            .pressButton('Log In', function(err) {
              if (err) throw err;
              assert.equal(browser.location.pathname, '/todos');
              next(browser, done);
            });
```

```
            });
        });
    };
};
```

This module makes sure that a test user exists before loading, filling, and posting the user login form. After that it hands off the control to a `next` function.

Testing the to-do list page

Now we are ready to add further description scopes inside our `todos` scope. One of these scopes is the to-do list, which will have this code:

```
describe('Todo list', function() {

    it('should have core elements', login(function(browser, done) {
        assert.equal(browser.text('h1'), 'Your To-Dos');
        assert(browser.query('a[href="/todos/new"]'),
            'should have a link to create a new Todo');
        assert.equal(browser.text('a[href="/todos/new"]'), 'New To-Do');
        done();
    }));


    it('should start with an empty list', login(function(browser,
done) {
        assert.equal(browser.queryAll('#todo-list tr').length, 0,
            'To-do list length should be 0');
        done();
    }));


    it('should not load when the user is not logged in',
function(done) {
        Browser.visit('http://localhost:3000/todos', function(err,
browser) {
            if (err) throw err;
            assert.equal(browser.location.pathname, '/session/new',
                'should be redirected to login screen');
            done();
        });
    });

});
```

Here we can see that that we are making use of our `login` module to abstract away the session initiation dance, making sure our callback function only gets called once the user is logged in. Here we have three tests.

In our first test, named `should have core elements`, we are simply loading the empty to-do list and asserting that we have some elements in place, such as a heading containing the `Your To-dos` text and a link to create a new to-do item.

In the following test, named `should start with an empty list`, we are simply testing whether the to-do list contains zero elements.

In the last test of this scope, named `should not load when the user is not logged in`, we are asserting that this list is inaccessible to the user that has not yet initiated the session, making sure he is redirected to `/session/new` if we try to load the `To-do list` URL.

Testing the to-do item creation

Now, we need to test whether the to-do items can really be created. For that, follow these steps:

1. We need a new description scope that we'll name `Todo creation form`—which will be another subscope of the `Todos` one:

   ```
   describe('Todo creation form', function() {
   ```

2. We can now test whether the to-do creation form is available for the user who is not logged in:

   ```
   it('should not load when the user is not logged in',
   function(done) {
       Browser.visit('http://localhost:3000/todos/new',
   function(err, browser) {
           if (err) throw err;
           assert.equal(browser.location.pathname, '/session/new',
             'should be redirected to login screen');
           done();
       });
   });
   ```

Here we are verifying that the user gets redirected to the login screen if an attempt is made to load the to-do item creation form without being logged in.

3. If the user is logged in, we check whether the page loads with some expected elements such as the title and the form elements for creating a new to-do item:

```
it('should load with title and form', login(function(browser,
done) {
    browser.visit('http://localhost:3000/todos/new',
function(err) {
        if (err) throw err;
        assert.equal(browser.text('h1'), 'New To-Do');

        var form = browser.query('form');
        assert(form, 'should have a form');
        assert.equal(form.method, 'POST', 'form should use post');
        assert.equal(form.action, '/todos', 'form should post to /
todos');

        assert(browser.query('textarea[name=what]', form),
          'should have a what textarea input');
        assert(browser.query('input[type=submit]', form),
          'should have an input submit type');

        done();
    });
}));
```

Here we are verifying that the form is present, that it has the necessary attributes to make a POST request to the /todos URL, and that the form has a text area input and a button to press.

4. Now we can also test whether we can successfully create a to-do item by filling the respective form and submitting it:

```
it('should allow to create a todo', login(function(browser,
done) {
    browser.visit('http://localhost:3000/todos/new',
function(err) {
        if (err) throw err;

        browser
          .fill('What', 'Laundry')
          .pressButton('Create', function(err) {
            if (err) throw err;
```

```
            assert.equal(browser.location.pathname, '/todos',
              'should be redirected to /todos after creation');

            var list = browser.queryAll('#todo-list tr.todo');
            assert.equal(list.length, 1, 'To-do list length should
  be 1');
            var todo = list[0];
            assert.equal(browser.text('td.pos', todo), 1);
            assert.equal(browser.text('td.what', todo),
  'Laundry');

            done();

          });
        });
      }));
```

Here we are finally testing whether the form allows us to post a new item and whether the item gets created. We are doing that by loading and filling in the to-do item creation form; verifying that we've been redirected to the to-do item list page; and that this page contains the single to-do item that we've just created.

Testing to-do item removal

Now that we've tested to-do item insertion, we can test whether one can actually remove these items from one's list. We will place these tests inside a describe scope named `Todo removal form`, inside which we will test for two things: the removal of one to-do item when only one exists and the removal of a to-do item when more than one item exists.

 We are doing these two tests separately because it's easier to understand the one-item test and then move on to the more complex one and also to test separately that we are not making off-by-one errors that are so common in programming.

Here is the code for the removal from a one-item list:

```
describe('Todo removal form', function() {

  describe('When one todo item exists', function() {
```

```
beforeEach(function(done) {
  // insert one todo item
  db.insert(fixtures.todo, fixtures.user.email, done);
});

it("should allow you to remove", login(function(browser, done) {

  browser.visit('http://localhost:3000/todos', function(err,
browser) {
    if (err) throw err;

    assert.equal(browser.queryAll('#todo-list tr.todo').length,
1);

    browser.pressButton('#todo-list tr.todo .remove form
input[type=submit]',
      function(err) {
        if (err) throw err;
        assert.equal(browser.location.pathname, '/todos');
        // assert that all todos have been removed
        assert.equal(browser.queryAll('#todo-list tr').length, 0);
        done();
      }
    );

  });
}));

});
```

Before we run the test, there is a `beforeEach` hook that inserts a to-do item into the `todo` database for the test user. That's just one to-do item that's taken from `fixtures.todo`, which is a property we need to add to the `test/fixtures.json` file:

```
{
  "user" : {
    "email": "me@email.com",
    "password": "mypassword"
  },
  "todo": {
    "todos": [
      {
```

```json
        "what": "Do the laundry",
        "created_at": 1346542066308
      }
    ]
  },
  "todos": {
    "todos": [
      {
        "what": "Do the laundry",
        "created_at": 1346542066308
      },
      {
        "what": "Call mom",
        "created_at": 1346542066308
      },
      {
        "what": "Go to gym",
        "created_at": 1346542066308
      }

    ]
  }

}
```

You may notice that, we're taking the opportunity here to add some additional fixtures that will help in future tests.

Continuing analyzing the test code, we see that the test fetches the to-do list and then verifies that the number of to-do items is actually one:

```
assert.equal(browser.queryAll('#todo-list tr.todo').length, 1);
```

Then it goes on to try and press the remove button of that one to-do item:

```
browser.pressButton('#todo-list tr.todo .remove form
input[type=submit]', …
```

The selector assumes that there is one to-do item on the table, which we had already verified before.

 If the browser cannot find a button or submit element from the given CSS selector, it will throw an error, ending the current test.

Then, after pressing the button and submitting the removal form, we're verifying that no errors occurred, that the browser was redirected back to the /todos URL, and that the presented list is now empty:

```
assert.equal(browser.queryAll('#todo-list tr').length, 0);
```

Now that we've tested that this works well for removing one item from a one-item list, let's create a more evolved test that asserts that we can remove a specific item from a list of three items:

```
describe('When more than one todo item exists', function() {

  beforeEach(function(done) {
    // insert one todo item
    db.insert(fixtures.todos, fixtures.user.email, done);
  });

  it("should allow you to remove one todo item", login(
    function(browser, done) {

      browser.visit('http://localhost:3000/todos', function(err,
browser) {
        if (err) throw err;

        var expectedList = [
          fixtures.todos.todos[0],
          fixtures.todos.todos[1],
          fixtures.todos.todos[2]
        ];

        var list = browser.queryAll('#todo-list tr');
        assert.equal(list.length, 3);

        list.forEach(function(todoRow, index) {
          assert.equal(browser.text('.pos', todoRow), index + 1);
          assert.equal(browser.text('.what', todoRow),
            expectedList[index].what);
        });
```

```
browser.pressButton(
  '#todo-list tr:nth-child(2) .remove input[type=submit]',
  function(err) {
    if (err) throw err;

    assert.equal(browser.location.pathname, '/todos');

    // assert that the middle todo item has been removed
    var list = browser.queryAll('#todo-list tr');
    assert.equal(list.length, 2);

    // remove the middle element from the expected list
    expectedList.splice(1,1);

    // test that the rendered list is the expected list
    list.forEach(function(todoRow, index) {
      assert.equal(browser.text('.pos', todoRow), index + 1);
      assert.equal(browser.text('.what', todoRow),
        expectedList[index].what);
    });

    done();
  }
);

        });
      }
    ));

  });
```

This description scope will sit at the same level as the previous one, also inserting a document in the todo database, but this time the document contains a list of three to-do items, taken from the fixtures.todos attribute (instead of the previously used singular fixtures.todo attribute).

The test starts by visiting the `todo` list page and building a list of the expected to-do items, stored in the variable named `expectedList`. We then retrieve all the to-do list items found on the HTML document and verify that the content is what is expected:

```
list.forEach(function(todoRow, index) {
  assert.equal(browser.text('.pos', todoRow), index + 1);
  assert.equal(browser.text('.what', todoRow),
    expectedList[index].what);
});
```

Once we have verified that all the expected to-do items are in place and in order, we go on to click on the button for the second item on the list by using the following code:

```
browser.pressButton(
  '#todo-list tr:nth-child(2) .remove input[type=submit]', ...
```

Here, we're using the special CSS selector `nth-child` for selecting exactly the row for the second do-to item and then fetching the code for removing submit button inside it, and finally pressing it.

Once the button is pressed, the form is submitted, and the browser calls back, we verify that there are no errors, that we got redirected back to the `/todos` URL, and also that it contains the expected list. We do this last bit by removing the second element from the previously used `expectedList` array and verifying that this is exactly what is shown in the current page:

```
var list = browser.queryAll('#todo-list tr');
assert.equal(list.length, 2);
expectedList.splice(1,1);

// test that the rendered list is the expected list
list.forEach(function(todoRow, index) {
  assert.equal(browser.text('.pos', todoRow), index + 1);
  assert.equal(browser.text('.what', todoRow),
    expectedList[index].what);
});
```

Putting it all together

You can run the tests individually by hand, but you should be able to run them all at once. For that, you simply need to call from the shell command line:

```
$ ./node_modules/.bin/mocha test/users.js test/session.js test/todos.js
```

We now need to change `package.json` so that you can inform **node package manager (npm)** how to run the tests:

```
{
  "description": "To-do App",
  "version": "0.0.0",
  "private": true,
  "dependencies": {
    "union": "0.3.0",
    "flatiron": "0.2.8",
    "plates": "0.4.x",
    "node-static": "0.6.0",
    "nano": "3.3.0",
    "flatware-cookie-parser": "0.1.x",
    "flatware-session": "0.1.x"
  },
  "devDependencies": {
    "mocha": "1.4.x",
    "zombie": "1.4.x"
  },
  "scripts": {
    "test": "mocha test/users.js test/session.js test/todos.js",
    "start": "node app.js"
  },
  "name": "todo",
  "author": "Pedro",
  "homepage": ""
}
```

You can now run your tests using:

```
$ npm test
   ............


   ✔ 13 tests complete (3758ms)
```

Summary

Zombie.js allows us to visit URLs, load HTML documents, and retrieve HTML elements using CSS selectors. It also allows us to easily fill forms and submit them, to click on buttons and follow links, to verify the return status code, and to analyze the response document in the same way using a terse, convenient API.

6
Testing Interactions

So far we have tested the filling of text fields on a form, but there are other more complex input fields that you can instruct a Zombie browser to fill.

For instance, you may want to select a radio button element, or choose one item from a drop-down list box, or you may want to select a particular date from a date input field.

When interacting with form fields and other elements, your application may manipulate the document—to show or hide some elements, for instance. By the end of this chapter you will know how to use Zombie.js to validate the effects of manipulating the document with JavaScript.

The topics covered in this chapter are:

- How to trigger changes in other form objects
- How to test DOM manipulations

Acting on radio buttons

To test the usage of radio buttons, we need to add some to a form in our app. We will introduce a radio button in the to-do item creation form to indicate if an alarm should be scheduled. Depending on the selected value, a field should appear, allowing us to set the to-do item's alarm date and time.

1. First, we need to change the to-do item creation template in `templates/todos/new.html` to:

```
<h1>New To-Do</h1>
<form id="new-todo-form" action="/todos" method="POST">
```

```
<p>
  <label for="what">What</label>
  <textarea name="what" id="what" required></textarea>
</p>

<p>

  <label class="radio" for="alarm-false">
    <input type="radio" name="alarm" value="false" id="alarm-
false" checked="checked" /> No Alarm
  </label>

  <label class="radio" for="alarm-true">
    <input type="radio" name="alarm" value="true" id="alarm-
true" /> Use Alarm
  </label>

</p>

<div id="alarm-date-time" style="display:none">
  <label class="date" for="alarm-date">
    <input type="text" name="alarm-date" id="alarm-date" /> Date
(YYYY/MM/DD)
  </label>
  <label class="time" for="alarm-time">
    <input type="text" name="alarm-time" id="alarm-time" /> Time
(hh:mm)
  </label>
</div>

<input type="submit" value="Create" />
</form>
```

2. This will present users with a couple of new radio buttons in the to-do item creation form:

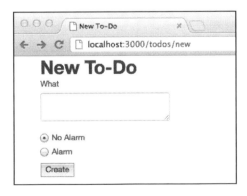

3. Now we also need to introduce some styles. Create a custom style sheet under `public/css/todo.css`:

```css
#alarm-date-time {
  position: relative;
  margin: 15px 0;
  padding: 39px 19px 14px;
  border: 1px solid #DDD;
  -webkit-border-radius: 4px;
  -moz-border-radius: 4px;
  border-radius: 4px;
  width: auto;
}

#alarm-date-time::after {
  content: "Alarm Date and time";
  position: absolute;
  top: -1px;
  left: -1px;
  padding: 3px 7px;
  font-size: 12px;
  font-weight: bold;
  background-color: whiteSmoke;
  border: 1px solid #DDD;
  color: #9DA0A4;
  -webkit-border-radius: 4px 0 4px 0;
  -moz-border-radius: 4px 0 4px 0;
  border-radius: 4px 0 4px 0;
}
```

4. We need to refer the previous CSS file in our layout file in `templates/layout.html`:

```html
<html>
  <head>
    <meta http-equiv="Content-Type" content="text/html; charset=utf-8" />
    <title id="title"></title>
    <link href="/css/bootstrap.min.css" rel="stylesheet" >
    <link href="/css/todo.css" rel="stylesheet" >
  </head>
  <body>
```

```
<section role="main" class="container">

  <div id="messages"></div>

  <div id="main-body"></div>

</section>

<script src="/js/jquery.min.js"></script>
<script src="/js/jquery-ui-1.8.23.custom.min.js"></script>
<script src="/js/bootstrap.min.js"></script>
<script src="/js/todos.js"></script>
</body>
</html>
```

5. Next we need to make the date and time form fields appear when the user selects the **Alarm** radio button. For that we need to introduce an event listener in the public/js/todos.js file:

```
$(function() {
  $('#todo-list').sortable({
    update: function() {
      var order = [];
      $('.todo').each(function(idx, row) {
        order.push($(row).find('.pos').text());
      });

      $.post('/todos/sort', {order: order.join(',')}, function() {
        $('.todo').each(function(idx, row) {
          $(row).find('.pos').text(idx + 1);
        });
      });
    }

  }
});

function hideOrShowDateTime() {
  var ringAlarm = $('input[name=alarm]:checked',
    '#new-todo-form').val() === 'true';
```

```
  if (ringAlarm) {
    $('#alarm-date-time').slideDown();
  } else {
    $('#alarm-date-time').slideUp();
  }
}

  $('#new-todo-form input[name=alarm]').
change(hideOrShowDateTime);
  hideOrShowDateTime();

});
```

This new event listener will listen for changes in the radio button and then hide or show the alarm date and time fields accordingly, resulting in the following screen when the Alarm setting is turned on:

6. We also need to change the route listener for the form post to accommodate these new fields:

```
this.post('/', [loggedIn, function() {

  var req  = this.req,
      res  = this.res,
      todo = this.req.body
  ;

  if (! todo.what) {
    res.writeHead(200, {'Content-Type': 'text/html'});
    return res.end(layout(templates['new'], 'New To-Do',
      {error: 'Please fill in the To-Do description'}));
  }

  todo.alarm = todo.alarm === 'true';
  todo.alarm_date = Date.parse(todo['alarm-date'] + ' ' +
todo['alarm-time']);
  delete todo['alarm-date'];
  delete todo['alarm-time'];

  todo.created_at = Date.now();

  insert(req.session.user.email, todo, function(err) {

    if (err) {
      res.writeHead(500);
      return res.end(err.stack);
    }

    res.writeHead(303, {Location: '/todos'});
    res.end();
  });

}]);
```

This new piece of code processes the alarm date and alarm time submitted in the form fields and parses them into a timestamp. A to-do item contained in the todo variable is then converted into a document that looks like this:

```
{ what: 'Deliver books to library',
  alarm: true,
  alarm_date: 1351608900000,
  created_at: 1350915191244 }
```

Testing the user interaction

For testing these new form fields and their combined behavior, we will use the test file in `test/todos.js`, and augment the `Todo creation form` scope:

1. First we test that these radio buttons do exist and that the alarms are turned off by default:

```
it('should not present the alarm date form fields when no alarm is
selected',
   login(function(browser, done) {
      browser.visit('http://localhost:3000/todos/new',
function(err) {
         if (err) throw err;

         browser.choose('No Alarm', function(err) {
            if (err) throw err;

            assert.equal(browser.query('#alarm-date-time').style.
display, 'none');
            done();
         });
      });
   })
);
```

Here we're verifying that we actually have two radio buttons for the `alarm` field, one having a `false` and the other having a `true` string value. Then we also verify that the first one is checked.

2. We also need to verify that the animation of the new date and time form fields works; the `div` element that wraps the alarm date and time input fields should be hidden when the user chooses not to use the alarm. When the user selects the `Use alarm` radio button, the `div` element should then be made visible:

```
it('should present the alarm date form fields when alarm',
   login(function(browser, done) {
      browser.visit('http://localhost:3000/todos/new', function(err)
{
         if (err) throw err;

         var container = browser.query('#alarm-date-time');

         browser.choose('No Alarm', function(err) {
            if (err) throw err;
```

```
      assert.equal(container.style.display, 'none');

      browser.choose('Use Alarm', function(err) {
        if (err) throw err;

        assert.equal(container.style.display, '');

        browser.choose('No Alarm', function(err) {
          if (err) throw err;

          assert.equal(container.style.display, 'none');

          done();
        });
      });
    });
  });
 })
);
```

Here, we are turning the use alarm setting on and off and verifying that the style of the container, `div`, changes accordingly. In Zombie, all the user interaction functions (such as `browser.choose()`, `browser.fill()`, and others) allow you to pass in a callback function as the last argument. This function will be invoked once the browser event loop is free, which means that your function will only be invoked after any animation. This is really useful since your test code doesn't have to explicitly wait for the animation to finish. You can be assured that the DOM is manipulated once your callback function gets called.

Using this technique, you can also test for any user interaction. By providing a callback function that Zombie invokes when all the actions are complete, you can test the effect that those actions had on the document.

In our case, we tested that we succeed in changing the style attribute of a `div` element, but you can also test other interactions using this technique. For instance, as we'll see in the next chapter, we can test that the content has changed according to some user actions.

Selecting values

If you have a select box in a form, you can also instruct Zombie to select a list item for you. Let's change our to-do item creation form to include an additional select box that describes the scope of the item—whether the item is related to work, family, or if it's a personal task.

First, we need to introduce this additional field into the to-do item creation form in `templates/todos/new.html`, right after the `What` text area field:

```
<label for="scope">
  Scope
  <select name="scope" id="scope">
    <option value="" selected="selected">Please select</option>
    <option value="work">Work</option>
    <option value="personal">Personal</option>
    <option value="family">Family</option>
  </select>
</label>
```

This will present the following form containing the additional **Scope** label and a select box:

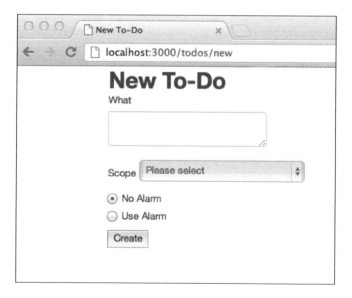

Now we need to have a test that verifies that this form contains the `select` element and the `option` items. For that, let's keep extending the file in `test/todos.js`, inside the `Todo creation form` description scope:

```
it('should present the scope select box',
  login(function(browser, done) {
    browser.visit('http://localhost:3000/todos/new', function(err) {
      if (err) throw err;

      var select = browser.queryAll('form select[name=scope]');
      assert.equal(select.length, 1);

      var options = browser.queryAll('form select[name=scope]
option');
      assert.equal(options.length, 4);

      options = options.map(function(option) {
        return [option.value, option.textContent];
      });

      var expectedOptions = [
        [null, 'Please select'],
        ['work', 'Work'],
        ['personal', 'Personal'],
        ['family', 'Family']
      ];

      assert.deepEqual(options, expectedOptions);

      done();

    });
  })
);
```

Here we're testing that the `select` element exists, that it has four `option` items, and that each item has the expected value and text.

Now we need to change the to-do list to present this new scope field. For that, we need to introduce it in the `templates/todos/index.html` file:

```html
<h1>Your To-Dos</h1>

<a class="btn" href="/todos/new">New To-Do</a>

<table class="table">
  <thead>
    <tr>
      <th>#</th>
      <th>What</th>
      <th>Scope</th>
      <th></th>
    </tr>
  </thead>
  <tbody id="todo-list">
    <tr class="todo">
      <td class="pos"></td>
      <td class="what"></td>
      <td class="scope"></td>
      <td class="remove">
        <form action="/todos/delete" method="POST">
          <input type="hidden" name="pos" value="" />
          <input type="submit" name="Delete" value="Delete" />
        </form>
      </td>
    </tr>
  </tbody>
</table>
```

We also need to fill the value when presenting the to-do item list in the `routes/todos.js` file, in the `GET` `/` route listener:

```javascript
this.get('/', [loggedIn, function() {

  var res = this.res;

  db.get(this.req.session.user.email, function(err, todos) {
```

```
if (err && err.status_code !== 404) {
  res.writeHead(500);
  return res.end(err.stack);
}

if (! todos) todos = {todos: []};
todos = todos.todos;

todos.forEach(function(todo, idx) {
  if (todo) todo.pos = idx + 1;
});

var map = Plates.Map();
map.className('todo').to('todo');
map.className('pos').to('pos');
map.className('what').to('what');
map.className('scope').to('scope');
map.where('name').is('pos').use('pos').as('value');

var main = Plates.bind(templates.index, {todo: todos}, map);
res.writeHead(200, {'Content-Type': 'text/html'});
res.end(layout(main, 'To-Dos'));

});
```

This will result in a to-do list like the one shown in the following screenshot, where the scope attribute of each to-do item is presented:

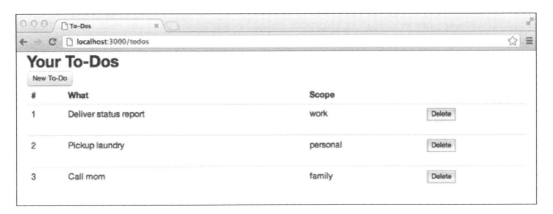

Now we need to test that the to-do item creation succeeds in capturing the scope value. For this, we'll slightly change the test named should allow to create a todo:

```
it('should allow to create a todo', login(function(browser, done) {
  browser.visit('http://localhost:3000/todos/new', function(err) {
    if (err) throw err;

    browser
      .fill('What', 'Laundry')
      .select('scope', 'Personal')
      .pressButton('Create', function(err) {
        if (err) throw err;

        assert.equal(browser.location.pathname, '/todos',
          'should be redirected to /todos after creation');

        var list = browser.queryAll('#todo-list tr.todo');
        assert.equal(list.length, 1, 'To-do list length should be 1');
        var todo = list[0];
        assert.equal(browser.text('td.pos', todo), 1);
        assert.equal(browser.text('td.what', todo), 'Laundry');
        assert.equal(browser.text('td.scope', todo), 'personal');

        done();

      });
  });
}));
```

Summary

Zombie allows you to manipulate any form object including text fields, text areas, select boxes, checkboxes and radio buttons.

Zombie not only allows the testing of server responses, but also the simulation of user interaction. If your application dynamically changes the document when a user event is triggered (such as selecting an option or clicking on an element), using Zombie and browser queries, you can verify that the behavior is as intended.

Even when user-triggered animations are present (such as fade-in), Zombie will not invoke the callback until these animations are complete.

In the next chapter, we will analyze how we can use Zombie.js to test user interactions that perform the AJAX calls.

7
Debugging

This chapter shows how you can use the browser object to inspect some internal states of your application.

Topics covered in this chapter include:

- Enabling the debugging output
- Dumping the browser state

By default, Zombie does not output the internal events to the console, but you can run Zombie with the DEBUG environment variable set to true. If you have a UNIX shell command line, you can prefix the launching of your test suite with DEBUG=true, shown as follows:

```
$ DEBUG=true node_modules/.bin/mocha test/todos
```

If you are running Windows, you can set and unset the DEBUG environment variable shown as follows:

```
$ SET DEBUG=true
$ SET DEBUG=
```

By enabling this environment variable, Zombie will output every HTTP request that it makes, along with the received HTTP status code:

```
...
Zombie: GET http://localhost:3000/js/todos.js => 200
Zombie: 303 => http://localhost:3000/todos
Zombie: GET http://localhost:3000/todos => 200
Zombie: GET http://localhost:3000/js/jquery-1.8.2.js => 200
```

```
Zombie: GET http://localhost:3000/js/jquery-ui.js => 200

Zombie: GET http://localhost:3000/js/todos.js => 200

Zombie: GET http://localhost:3000/js/bootstrap.min.js => 200

...
```

 As you can see, Zombie also reports all the `3xx-class` HTTP redirects and what the new URL is.

This output may be helpful for debugging some URL loading problems, but it can be hard to track down which test a specific HTTP request is referring to.

Fortunately, there is a way to bring some clarification to the test output by changing the Mocha reporter. Mocha comes with a feature called reporters. So far we've used the default reporter, which reports a colored point for every test. But if you specify the `spec` reporter, Mocha outputs the test name right before the test starts and right after the test ends.

To enable the `spec` reporter, just add `-R spec` to the Mocha arguments shown as follows:

```
$ DEBUG=true node_modules/.bin/mocha -R spec test/todos
```

This way you will get an output that is similar to the following:

```
...
    . should start with an empty list: Zombie: GET http://
localhost:3000/session/new => 200

Zombie: GET http://localhost:3000/js/jquery-1.8.2.js => 200

Zombie: GET http://localhost:3000/js/jquery-ui.js => 200

Zombie: GET http://localhost:3000/js/bootstrap.min.js => 200

Zombie: GET http://localhost:3000/js/todos.js => 200

Zombie: 302 => http://localhost:3000/todos

Zombie: GET http://localhost:3000/todos => 200

Zombie: GET http://localhost:3000/js/jquery-1.8.2.js => 200

Zombie: GET http://localhost:3000/js/jquery-ui.js => 200

Zombie: GET http://localhost:3000/js/todos.js => 200

Zombie: GET http://localhost:3000/js/bootstrap.min.js => 200

    ✓ should start with an empty list (378ms)

    . should not load when the user is not logged in: Zombie: 303 =>
http://localhost:3000/session/new
```

```
Zombie: GET http://localhost:3000/session/new => 200

Zombie: GET http://localhost:3000/js/jquery-1.8.2.js => 200

Zombie: GET http://localhost:3000/js/jquery-ui.js => 200

Zombie: GET http://localhost:3000/js/bootstrap.min.js => 200

Zombie: GET http://localhost:3000/js/todos.js => 200
        ✓ should not load when the user is not logged in (179ms)
...
```

This not only tells you which resource loads corresponding to a given test, it also informs you of how much time was spent running that test.

Running a specific test

If you are having trouble with a specific test, you don't need to run the whole test suite or even the whole test file. Mocha accepts a -g <expression> command-line option, and will only run the tests that match that expression.

For instance, you can run only the tests that have the word remove in the description, shown as follows:

```
$ DEBUG=true node_modules/.bin/mocha -R spec -g 'remove' test/todos


  Todos
    Todo removal form
      When one todo item exists
        ◦ should allow you to remove: Zombie: GET http://localhost:3000/
session/new => 200
...
        ✓ should allow you to remove (959ms)
      When more than one todo item exists
        ◦ should allow you to remove one todo item: Zombie: GET http://
localhost:3000/session/new => 200
...
        ✓ should allow you to remove one todo item (683ms)


  ✔ 2 tests complete (1780ms)
```

This way you will be running only these specific tests.

Enabling the debugging output per test

Setting the DEBUG environment variable to true enables debugging output for all tests, but you can instead specify which tests you want to debug, by setting browser.debug to true. For instance, change the test/todos.js file and around line 204 add this:

```
    ...
        it("should allow you to remove", login(function(browser, done) {
            browser.debug = true;

            browser.visit('http://localhost:3000/todos', function(err,
    browser) {
    ...
```

This way you don't need to specify the DEBUG environment variable when running the following test:

```
$ node_modules/.bin/mocha -R spec -g 'remove' test/todos


  Todos
    Todo removal form
      When one todo item exists
        . should allow you to remove: Zombie: GET http://localhost:3000/
todos => 200
Zombie: GET http://localhost:3000/js/jquery.min.js => 200
Zombie: GET http://localhost:3000/js/jquery-ui-1.8.23.custom.min.js =>
200
Zombie: GET http://localhost:3000/js/bootstrap.min.js => 200
Zombie: GET http://localhost:3000/js/todos.js => 200
Zombie: 303 => http://localhost:3000/todos
Zombie: GET http://localhost:3000/todos => 200
Zombie: GET http://localhost:3000/js/jquery.min.js => 200
Zombie: GET http://localhost:3000/js/jquery-ui-1.8.23.custom.min.js =>
200
Zombie: GET http://localhost:3000/js/bootstrap.min.js => 200
Zombie: GET http://localhost:3000/js/todos.js => 200
        ✓ should allow you to remove (1191ms)
      When more than one todo item exists
        ✓ should allow you to remove one todo item (926ms)
```

```
✔ 2 tests complete (2308ms)
```

Here you can see that, as intended, Zombie only outputs debugging information for the test named should allow you to remove.

Using the browser JavaScript console

Other than the HTTP requests that the browser makes, Zombie doesn't output much else that may be interesting or useful while debugging for you to debug your application.

A good option, which provides far more flexibility and insight, is to run your application inside a real browser with developer tools and/or a debugger.

A particularly useful alternative for debugging issues that are encountered specifically in Zombie.js is to use the console.log() function inside your browser code (the code that, in the case of this app, sits inside the public/js directory).

As an example, suppose that you were having a problem with the to-do creation form: the alarm option was not correctly triggering the show and hide option of the alarm option pane. For this, we can introduce the following console.log statement in the public/js/todos.js file, in order to inspect the value of the ringAlarm variable: function hideOrShowDateTime().

```
{
  var ringAlarm = $('input[name=alarm]:checked',
    '#new-todo-form').val() === 'true';

  console.log('\ntriggered hide or show. ringAlarm is ', ringAlarm);

  if (ringAlarm) {
    $('#alarm-date-time').slideDown();
  } else {
    $('#alarm-date-time').slideUp();
  }
}
```

This way, when you run the test, you will get the following output:

```
$ node_modules/.bin/mocha -R spec -g 'alarm' test/todos
```

```
Todos
  Todo creation form
    . should have an alarm option:
triggered hide or show. ringAlarm is  false


triggered hide or show. ringAlarm is  false


triggered hide or show. ringAlarm is  false
      ✓ should have an alarm option (625ms)
    . should present the alarm date form fields when alarm:
triggered hide or show. ringAlarm is  false


triggered hide or show. ringAlarm is  false


triggered hide or show. ringAlarm is  false


triggered hide or show. ringAlarm is  false


triggered hide or show. ringAlarm is  true


triggered hide or show. ringAlarm is  true


triggered hide or show. ringAlarm is  false


triggered hide or show. ringAlarm is  false
      ✓ should present the alarm date form fields when alarm (1641ms)



  ✔ 2 tests complete (2393ms)
```

Using this technique, you can then inspect the state of your application when
the tests are being run.

Dumping the browser state

You can also inspect the browser state by doing a `browser.dump()` function call inside your test code.

1. For instance, you may want to know the full browser state inside the `should present the alarm date form fields when alarm` test in the `test/todos.js` file. For this, introduce a `browser.dump()` call immediately after we choose the `No Alarm` option:

```
...
    it('should present the alarm date form fields when alarm',
      login(function(browser, done) {
        browser.visit('http://localhost:3000/todos/new',
function(err) {
          if (err) throw err;

          var container = browser.query('#alarm-date-time');

          browser.choose('No Alarm', function(err) {
            if (err) throw err;

            assert.equal(container.style.display, 'none');

            browser.choose('Use Alarm', function(err) {
              if (err) throw err;

              assert.equal(container.style.display, '');

              browser.choose('No Alarm', function(err) {
                if (err) throw err;

                browser.dump();

                assert.equal(container.style.display, 'none');

                done();
              });
            });
          });
        })
      })
    );
...
```

2. Make the change in the file and run this test:

```
$ node_modules/.bin/mocha -R spec -g 'alarm' test/todos
```

```
  Todos
    Todo creation form
      ✓ should have an alarm option (659ms)
      ◦ should present the alarm date form fields when alarm: Zombie:
1.4.1
```

URL: http://localhost:3000/todos/new

History:

1. http://localhost:3000/session/new

2. http://localhost:3000/todos

3: http://localhost:3000/todos/new

sid=AIUjSvUl79S8Qz4Q8foRRAS7; Domain=localhost; Path=/

Cookies:

true

Storage:

Eventloop:

The time: Mon Feb 18 2013 10:59:43 GMT+0000 (WET)

Timers: 0

Processing: 0

Waiting: 0

Document:

```html
  <html>
    <head>     <meta http-equiv="Content-Type" content="text/html;
charset=utf-8" />
      <title id="title">New To-Do</title>
      <link href="/css/bootstrap.min.css" rel="stylesheet" />
      <link href="/css/todo.css" rel="stylesheet" />
    </head>
```

```
    <body>    <section role="main" class="container">        <div
id="messages"></div>
        <div id="main-body">
        <h1>New To-Do</h1>
        <form id="new-todo-form" action="/todos" method="POST">
<p>        <label for="what">What<//...
```

✓ should present the alarm date form fields when alarm (1426ms)

✔ 2 tests complete (2236ms)

When performing a `browser.dump()` call, you will get the following in the output:

- The current URL
- The history, that is, all the URLs that this browser instance visited after creation
- The offline storage, if you use any
- The event loop state: if it's waiting on any processing or timers
- The first lines of the HTML document, which may be enough to debug the current state

Dumping the whole document

If at any time you need to inspect the entire contents of your document, you can inspect the return value of `browser.html()`. For instance, if you want to inspect the document's state right before the browser is reloaded, you can add the following line to the `test/todo.js` file, in place of `browser.dump()`:

```
...
        browser.choose('Use Alarm', function(err) {
          if (err) throw err;

          assert.equal(container.style.display, '');

          browser.choose('No Alarm', function(err) {
            if (err) throw err;

            console.log(browser.html());
```

```
                    assert.equal(container.style.display, 'none');

                    done();
                });
            });
    ...
```

You can now run the test and observe the output:

```
$ node_modules/.bin/mocha -g 'alarm' test/todos
...
  <html style=""><head>

...
```

Summary

Your browser developer tools are better suited for debugging your browser application. However, if you run into Zombie-specific issues, there are several techniques that may help you.

One is to enable the Zombie debugging output. This will show you which resources the browser is loading and what the corresponding response status codes that are shown alongside are.

You can run specific tests. When debugging a specific problem in a test, you can also restrict Mocha to run only that test by using the `-g <pattern>` option.

You can use the `console.log` command in the code that runs in the browser; the output will appear in the console.

You can view the current browser state. You can inspect the browser state by using the `browser.dump` call, or by logging the result of `browser.html` to the console.

If you need to access the whole document at some stage of your test, you can also log the return value of `browser.html()`.

8
Testing AJAX

In this book, we have tested the filling of text fields on a form, clicking on buttons, and the resulting HTML document. This makes us ready to test a traditional form-based request-response application, but typical modern applications are usually more complex than that as they make use of asynchronous HTTP requests, that somehow update the document without having to refresh it. This is because they use AJAX.

Our application emits AJAX requests when presented with the to-do item list page; a user can drag an item and drop it in the new position. The code that we placed in the `public/js/todos.js` file catches the change and calls the server `/todos/sort` URL, changing the item order in the database.

Let's see how we can use Zombie to test this drag-and-drop feature. The topics covered in this chapter include:

- Using Zombie to trigger an AJAX call
- Using Zombie to test the result of an AJAX call

By the end of this section, you will know how to use Zombie to test an application that uses AJAX.

Implementing drag-and-drop

Let's add some tests to the `test/todos.js` file.

1. We start off by adding a new describe scope before the end of the `Todo list` scope:

   ```
   describe('When there are some items on the list', function() {
   ```

   This new scope allows us to setup a to-do item fixture list in the database before any test inside this scope is run.

2. Now, let's add this new `beforeEach` hook inside the new scope:

```
beforeEach(function(done) {
  // insert todo items
  db.insert(fixtures.todos, fixtures.user.email, done);
});
```

3. Then we start the test by logging in:

```
it('should allow me to reorder items using drag and drop',
  login(function(browser, done) {
```

4. We start the test by making sure that we have three to-do items in our item list page:

```
var items = browser.queryAll('#todo-list tr');
assert.equal(items.length, 3, 'Should have 3 items and has ' +
  items.length);
```

5. Then we declare a helper function that will assist us in verifying the contents of that list:

```
function expectOrder(order) {
  var itemTexts = browser.queryAll('#todo-list tr .what').map(
    function(node) {
      return node.textContent.trim();
    }   assert.equal(index + 1, itemPos);
  });
}
```

This function gets an array of strings and asserts that the `what` and `pos` fields of each to-do item in the page are placed in the expected order.

6. Then we use this new `expectOrder` function to actually test that the order is the expected one:

```
expectOrder(['Do the laundry', 'Call mom', 'Go to gym']);
```

As you may remember, this is the order of the to-do items as declared in the `test/fixtures.json` file that were loaded on the `beforeEach` hook.

7. Next we create another helper function that will help us fabricate and inject mouse events:

```
function mouseEvent(name, target, x, y) {
  var event = browser.document.createEvent('MouseEvents');
  event.initEvent(name, true, true);
  event.clientX = event.screenX = x;
  event.clientY = event.screenY = y;
  event.which = 1;
  browser.dispatchEvent(item, event);
}
```

This function simulates a user mouse event, sets the x and y coordinates on it, sets the mouse button (`event.which = 1`), and dispatches the event into the browser, specifying which item the event happened on.

8. Next we select which to-do item we will be dragging; in this case, we drag the first one:

```
var item = items[0];
```

9. Then we use the `mouseEvent` helper function to inject a sequence of fabricated events:

```
mouseEvent('mousedown', item, 50, 50);
mouseEvent('mousemove', browser.document, 51, 51);
mouseEvent('mousemove', browser.document, 51, 150);
mouseEvent('mouseup',  browser.document, 51, 150);
```

There are several important aspects to these events, namely, the sequence of events, the target element, and the mouse coordinates. Let's analyze them.

These are the events that compose a drag and a drop. First we press the mouse button, we move it a bit, then we move it some more and finally we release the mouse button. The x and y values for the mouse event location we're using here aren't really important, what is important is the relative difference between them so that the drag is detected and the drag mode begins.

On the first event, the `mousedown`, we're using an arbitrary coordinate of `50`, `50`. On the second event, the `mousemove`, we're incrementing this coordinate by one pixel; this starts the drag.

The second `mousemove` event continues the drag on the y axis. It looks superfluous and redundant, but it's required so that the drag detection works, giving continuity to the drag movement we were performing.

Finally we have the `mouseup` where the user releases the mouse. This event uses the same coordinates as the previous `mousemove`, indicating that the user dropped the element after the drag.

Let's now analyze the target elements in the events:

The second argument of the `mouseEvent()` helper function takes the target element. In the first `mousedown` event injection, we're targeting the to-do item in the `item` variable, which refers the item we want to drag. This indicates which item we will be dragging, once the drag mode gets activated. The remaining three events target the browser document, since the user will be dragging the to-do item across the document.

Some further clarification of the mouse coordinates we're using:

Zombie does not render the items, so it doesn't know the location of each of them. This is the only way we can use to indicate which element we are dragging. The x and y coordinates in this case are irrelevant for that.

Since Zombie doesn't render the elements, it doesn't keep the location of each element. In fact, they are all placed at (0, 0), which means that our `mouseup` event placed the dragged item after the last item.

As mentioned earlier, the initial value and the drag distance is completely arbitrary, and you will find that changing these will still make the test work.

10. After injecting these mouse events into the browser event queue, we wait for these to be fully processed using `browser.wait()` function:

```
browser.wait(function(err) {
        if (err) throw err;
```

At this stage, the browser has changed the element order and made an AJAX request posting the new order to the server.

11. Now we verify that the to-do items are in the new order:

```
expectOrder(['Call mom', 'Go to gym', 'Do the laundry']);
```

12. We also verify whether the browser performed the HTTP request we intended:

```
var lastRequest = browser.lastRequest;
assert.equal(lastRequest.url, 'http://localhost:3000/todos/sort');
assert.equal(lastRequest.method, 'POST');
```

 Notice that we're using the browser.lastRequest() function to access the last AJAX request the browser made.
If you needed to access every HTTP request that the browser made, you can inspect the browser.resources object.

Now that we know that the browser made an HTTP POST request commanding that the server sorts the to-do items, we need to make sure the to-do items were correctly updated in the database. To verify this we do something similar to what a human tester would; we reload the page using browser.reload() and verify to see if the order is indeed the expected one:

```
browser.reload(function(err) {
  if (err) throw err;

  expectOrder(['Call mom', 'Go to gym', 'Do the laundry']);

  done();

});
```

Summary

Using Zombie you can inject custom events to imitate some complex user actions. You can also detect what URL and method the browser performed an HTTP request to by using browser.lastRequest().

Index

Thank you for buying
Using Node.js for UI Testing

About Packt Publishing

Packt, pronounced 'packed', published its first book "*Mastering phpMyAdmin for Effective MySQL Management*" in April 2004 and subsequently continued to specialize in publishing highly focused books on specific technologies and solutions.

Our books and publications share the experiences of your fellow IT professionals in adapting and customizing today's systems, applications, and frameworks. Our solution based books give you the knowledge and power to customize the software and technologies you're using to get the job done. Packt books are more specific and less general than the IT books you have seen in the past. Our unique business model allows us to bring you more focused information, giving you more of what you need to know, and less of what you don't.

Packt is a modern, yet unique publishing company, which focuses on producing quality, cutting-edge books for communities of developers, administrators, and newbies alike. For more information, please visit our website: www.packtpub.com.

About Packt Open Source

In 2010, Packt launched two new brands, Packt Open Source and Packt Enterprise, in order to continue its focus on specialization. This book is part of the Packt Open Source brand, home to books published on software built around Open Source licences, and offering information to anybody from advanced developers to budding web designers. The Open Source brand also runs Packt's Open Source Royalty Scheme, by which Packt gives a royalty to each Open Source project about whose software a book is sold.

Writing for Packt

We welcome all inquiries from people who are interested in authoring. Book proposals should be sent to author@packtpub.com. If your book idea is still at an early stage and you would like to discuss it first before writing a formal book proposal, contact us; one of our commissioning editors will get in touch with you.

We're not just looking for published authors; if you have strong technical skills but no writing experience, our experienced editors can help you develop a writing career, or simply get some additional reward for your expertise.

Node Web Development

ISBN: 978-1-849515-14-6   Paperback: 172 pages

A practical introduction to Node, the exciting new server-side JavaScript web development stack

1. Go from nothing to a database-backed web application in no time at all

2. Get started quickly with Node and discover that JavaScript is not just for browsers anymore

3. An introduction to server-side JavaScript with Node, the Connect and Express frameworks, and using SQL or MongoDB database back-end

Node Cookbook

ISBN: 978-1-849517-18-8   Paperback: 342 pages

Over 50 recipes to master the art of asynchronous server-side JavaScript using Node

1. Packed with practical recipes taking you from the basics to extending Node with your own modules

2. Create your own web server to see Node's features in action

3. Work with JSON, XML, web sockets, and make the most of asynchronous programming

Please check **www.PacktPub.com** for information on our titles

CoffeeScript Programming with jQuery, Rails, and Node.js

ISBN: 978-1-849519-58-8   Paperback: 140 pages

Learn CoffeeScript programming with the three most popular web technologies around

1. Learn CoffeeScript, a small and elegant language that compiles to JavaScript and will make your life as a web developer better

2. Explore the syntax of the language and see how it improves and enhances JavaScript

3. Build three example applications in CoffeeScript step by step

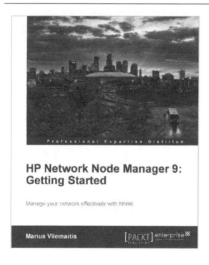

HP Network Node Manager 9: Getting Started

ISBN: 978-1-849680-84-4   Paperback: 584 pages

Manage your network effectively with NNMi

1. Install, customize, and expand NNMi functionality by developing custom features

2. Integrate NNMi with other management tools, such as HP SW Operations Manager, Network Automation, Cisco Works, Business Availability center, UCMDB, and many others

3. Navigate between incidents and maps to reduce troubleshooting time

Please check **www.PacktPub.com** for information on our titles

Made in the USA
San Bernardino, CA
25 March 2016